How to Use
MICROSOFT
WORD 97 FOR
WINDOWS

HEIDI STEELE

Ziff Davis Press
An imprint of Macmillan Computer Publishing USA
Emeryville, California

Publisher	Stacy Hiquet
Acquisitions Editor	Lysa Lewallen
Development Editor	Margo Hill
Copy Editor	Margo Hill
Technical Reviewer	Mark Hall
Project Coordinator	Edith Rex
Proofreader	Jeff Barash
Cover Illustration and Design	Megan Gandt
Book Design	Dennis Gallagher/Visual Strategies, San Francisco
Page Layout	Janet Piercy
Indexer	Valerie Robbins

Ziff-Davis Press, ZD Press, the Ziff-Davis Press logo PC Magazine, and the PC Magazine logo, PC Week and the PC Week logo are trademarks or registered trademarks of, and are licensed to Macmillan Computer Publishing USA by Ziff-Davis Publishing Company, New York, New York.

Ziff-Davis Press imprint books are produced on a Macintosh computer system with the following applications: FrameMaker®, Microsoft® Word, QuarkXPress®, Adobe Illustrator®, Adobe Photoshop®, Adobe Streamline™, MacLink®Plus, Aldus® FreeHand™, Collage Plus™.

Ziff-Davis Press, an imprint of
Macmillan Computer Publishing USA
5903 Christie Avenue
Emeryville, CA 94608

ISBN 1-56276-468-3

Manufactured in the United States of America
10 9 8 7 6 5 4 3 2 1

TABLE OF CONTENTS

ACKNOWLEDGMENTS

 Writing a computer book is very much a group effort, and I certainly have a long list of people to thank for their contributions to this project.

Lysa Lewallen helped launch the book and was always there to quickly resolve the inevitable glitches that occurred along the way. Edith Rex, project coordinator, efficiently shepherded all the chapters through the production process. Margo Hill, copy editor, lent her easygoing support throughout the project. And Mark Hall, technical reviewer, carefully checked the manuscript and helped research the obscure nooks and crannies of new features.

Thanks also to the other people at Ziff-Davis who brought their experience and expertise to the book: Sarah Ishida for the art work, Janet Piercy for page layout, Valerie Robbins for the index, and Jeff Barash for proofreading the manuscript. And Carol Burbo also deserves thanks for keeping track of everything.

Finally, I'd like to thank my parents Chuck and Candance, my sisters Danae and Heather, and my niece Thea for patiently listening to chatter about outlines, deadlines, and example documents, and to occasional ruminations on how to write and have a life at the same time.

INTRODUCTION

 How to Use Microsoft Word 97 for Windows is a book for beginners. It doesn't assume that you have experience using Word or any other word processing program. The concepts and skills that you will need to create effective and attractive documents in Word are explained from the ground up. However, this book does assume that you're comfortable with basic Windows 95 skills, such as using the mouse and working with menus and dialog boxes. If this is not the case, you might want to start with a beginning book on Windows 95, and then progress to Word once you have your bearings in the Windows 95 environment.

In this concise, colorful book, you will learn the simplest and most efficient ways of using Word. You will, of course, learn how to produce standard business documents—such as letters, memos, and reports. But unlike many beginning computer books, which avoid discussing more advanced topics for fear of intimidating the reader, this book assumes you are both intelligent and interested in getting the most out of Word. Therefore, you'll also be given the opportunity to learn about features such as tables, mail merge, graphics, and Web-page design.

The layout of this book is a little different from most other computer books. Rather than requiring you to wade through page after page of text to get to the "how to" information, this book presents information in bite-sized pieces, with plenty of pictures thrown in to help you follow along. Each chapter contains up to six related topics, and each topic spans two facing pages, so all the information you need is in front of you at one time. The material in each topic is presented in a series of numbered steps that revolve around a central graphic image, which is designed to reinforce the concepts at hand.

As you read through each chapter, you can type and work with the sample text if you like, but you don't need to. You can just as easily apply the directions in each topic to your own documents. This book is designed to work as both a hands-on tutorial and a reference.

While numbered steps explain the basics of carrying out each task, "Tip Sheets" in each topic also provide valuable shortcuts, alternative techniques for those of you who like variety, and helpful pointers on how to apply the skills to real documents.

You will find three "Try It" sections at strategic spots in this book. A Try It is a hands-on exercise that gives you valuable practice with the skills you've acquired up to that point. As you read these sections, be sure to follow each step at your computer.

To get the most out of How to Use Microsoft Word 97 for Windows, read the chapters in sequence. If you have any experience with Word or with word processing in general, you may already be familiar with some of the information presented in the first few chapters. However, the beginning chapters also contain tips and tricks you may not be aware of, and they introduce concepts that lay the foundation for the remaining chapters of the book.

CHAPTER 1

Welcome to Word for Windows

Microsoft Word is widely recognized as the best word processing program available. It is a powerful program, with plenty of advanced features that are worth exploring once you learn the basics. And it is so well designed that you won't feel overwhelmed by the large number of features. You don't have to wade through things you don't need to get to the commands you want. This chapter will introduce you to the Word interface and get you up to speed on the fundamental skills you'll use every time you work with Word.

You begin by learning how to start and exit Word. Then you get an introduction to the various elements of the Word window and to a few basic Windows concepts. Next, you learn a bit about typing in Word. Even if you have been using word processing programs for a while, you might want to glance over this topic to make sure you have the essentials under your belt. The last three topics teach you about document access: You learn how to save and close a document you've created, how to start a new document when Word is already open, and how to open a previously saved document to continue working on it.

This book is about Word 97 for Windows, so if you are using a previous version of Word, keep in mind that not all the features discussed in this book will apply to you.

How to Start and Exit Word

The main screen in Windows is called the *desktop*. The Windows desktop is displayed a few moments after you turn on your computer (and log in if you're on a network), and it remains open the entire time you're using the computer. When you start Word, the Word window displays on top of the desktop, and, depending on whether the window is maximized, may cover it completely.

TIP SHEET

▶ **You don't need to exit Word to use another program. If the program you want to use is already open, just click on its taskbar button at the bottom of your screen. If it's not open, you can open the program via the Start button. To go back to working in Word, click on its taskbar button.**

▶ **If you want to turn off your computer after exiting Word, you need to exit Windows itself. Click on the Start button and click on Shut Down. In the Shut Down Windows dialog box, click on the Yes button, then wait until you see the message "It's now safe to turn off your computer" before you turn off the computer. If you shut down Windows without closing Word and you have an unsaved document, you will be given a chance to save it.**

▶ **If you use Word extensively, you might want to create a shortcut icon for the program on your Windows desktop. To do this, display the MSOffice folder (either through the My Computer icon or through Windows Explorer), locate the Microsoft Word icon, and use the *right* mouse button to drag it onto the Windows desktop. Release the mouse, and choose Create Shortcut(s) Here from the context menu. You can then double-click on the shortcut icon to load Word.**

1 To start Word, begin by clicking the Start button in the lower-left corner of the Windows desktop. When you point to the Start button, a ScreenTip pops up to tell you about the button. You will see similar ScreenTips when you point to other buttons in Windows and in Word.

7 If you have an unsaved document, The Office Assistant asks whether you want to save it. (If you don't have the Office Assistant displayed, Word displays a simple message box asking the same question.) If you don't want to save the document, click on the No button; if you do, click on the Yes button, and refer to "How to Save and Close a Document" later in this chapter to complete the process of saving the document.

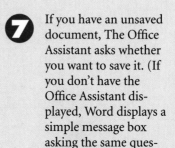

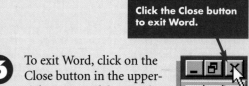

Click the Close button to exit Word.

6 To exit Word, click on the Close button in the upper-right corner of the Word window. If you see more than one Close button, click on the top one. (The lower Close button only closes the document you're working on; it doesn't close Word.) Alternatively, you can choose File, Exit.

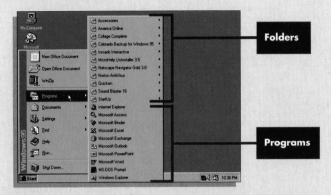

Folders

Programs

2 Move your mouse pointer over the Programs option to display a list of programs and folders, which in turn contain other programs and/or folders. (The programs and folders you see will differ from the ones shown here.)

3 Click on Microsoft Word to start the program. By default, Microsoft Word is included in the main Programs list, as shown here. If you don't see it, someone has probably customized your Start menu and placed Microsoft Word in a folder, so you might need to hunt around a bit to find it.

Word window

Windows desktop

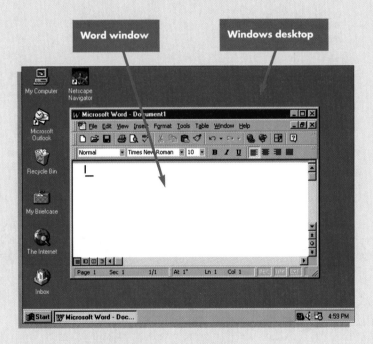

Office Assistant

4 Word loads with a blank document you can start typing in immediately. You may also see a small window with a paper clip figure (or another comical character such as a puppy or a bouncing ball). This is the Office Assistant, a new feature in Microsoft Office programs. It offers tips to help you in your work and gives you quick access to Word's online help system. You'll more about the Office Assistant in Chapter 3. In the meantime, you can either leave it open to see what it does, or close it by clicking its Close button (the X in the upper-right corner of the window).

Taskbar button

Taskbar

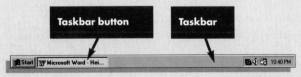

5 When Word is open, Windows displays a button with the name of the program in the taskbar at the bottom of the screen. The taskbar is normally displayed the entire time you're using Windows, and it shows which programs and My Computer folder windows you currently have open. If you don't see the taskbar on your screen, someone probably customized Windows to only show the taskbar when you move the mouse pointer to the bottom edge of the screen.

A Tour of the Word Window

When you start Word, you see the program window, named Microsoft Word, and one blank document window, named Document1. Usually, both windows are *maximized* (the program window fills the whole screen, and the document window fills the whole program window). When they are both maximized, two restore buttons, one for each window, are displayed in the set of buttons located in the upper-right corner of the screen (see the picture in the middle of the page). If you see a maximize button for either window, click on it. (The maximize button appears in place of the restore button; it looks like a single large square.) You'll probably find it preferable to keep both windows maximized, since it gives you more room to work.

▶ If you don't see the Standard or Formatting toolbar, or if you see other toolbars you'd like to hide, choose View, Toolbars. In the Toolbars dialog box, mark the check boxes for the Standard and Formatting toolbars and clear the check boxes for other toolbars, and then click on OK.

▶ If your scroll bars or status bar aren't showing, choose Tools, Options. Near the top of the Options dialog box, click on the View tab if it isn't already showing. Then, under Window, click on any option that isn't already marked—Status Bar, Horizontal Scroll Bar, and/or Vertical Scroll Bar—and then click on OK.

Program name   Document name

1 The title bar tells you what's in the window. When the document window is maximized, it has to share the title bar with the program window, so the title bar contains the names of both windows. If you restore the document window to a smaller size (by clicking its restore button), it gets its own separate title bar. Document1 is a temporary name for your document. When you save it for the first time, you replace that name with one of your choosing.

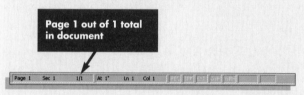

Page 1 out of 1 total in document

9 The status bar tells you what page you're on, the total number of pages, and where your insertion point is on the page. As you use Word, the status bar sometimes displays other information as well.

8 The Browse buttons (located in the lower-right corner of the document window) let you quickly jump from one part of your document to the next. (See Chapter 5 for more information.)

7 You use the View buttons (located in the lower-left corner of the document window) to change the way your document is displayed on screen. By default, Word uses Normal view. You'll learn about the different views in Chapter 4.

2 Word's menu bar contains nine menus. All the commands in Word are accessible through the menu system, so you don't have to use the toolbars and ruler if you don't want to.

3 To issue a menu command with your mouse, click on the menu name to display the menu, then click on the desired command. To issue a command with the keyboard, press the Alt key, and then press the underlined letter in the desired menu. (You can type the letter in upper- or lowercase.) To display the Format menu, for instance, you press Alt+O. Once the menu is displayed, press the underlined letter in the desired command. For example, press P to issue the Paragraph command.

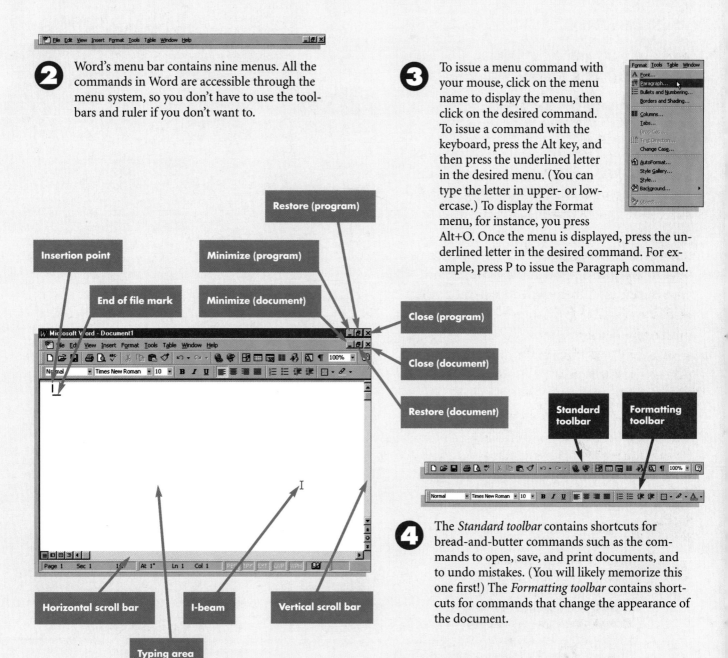

Restore (program)

Insertion point

Minimize (program)

End of file mark

Minimize (document)

Close (program)

Close (document)

Restore (document)

Standard toolbar

Formatting toolbar

Horizontal scroll bar

I-beam

Vertical scroll bar

Typing area

4 The *Standard toolbar* contains shortcuts for bread-and-butter commands such as the commands to open, save, and print documents, and to undo mistakes. (You will likely memorize this one first!) The *Formatting toolbar* contains shortcuts for commands that change the appearance of the document.

6 The typing area is blank except for three symbols. The *insertion point* (also known as the *cursor*) shows you where the next character you type will appear. The *end of file mark* shows you where the document ends. You use the mouse pointer to select text and to move the insertion point. When the mouse pointer is in the typing area, it becomes an *I-beam*.

5 The ruler shows you where your margins are, and it lets you set tabs and indents. If you don't see the ruler, you can temporarily bring it into view by resting the tip of your mouse pointer on the gray horizontal line directly underneath the Formatting toolbar. With this method, the ruler disappears as soon as you move the mouse pointer to another part of the screen. To keep the ruler constantly in view, choose View, Ruler. You'll find out more about using the ruler in Chapter 10.

How to Type Text in Word

When you start Word, you're presented with a blank document window, and you can begin typing right away. The flashing insertion point shows you where the next character you type will appear. You can move the insertion point to a new location by using the four arrow keys. You can also point a new location with your mouse, and then click once to move the insertion point. (See Chapter 5 for other ways to navigate in a document.)

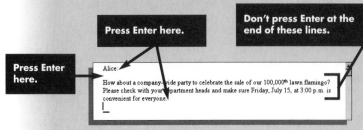

1 Each time you press Enter, you insert a *paragraph mark* into your document. Press Enter to end short lines of text, to create blank lines, and to end paragraphs. Do not press Enter to start new lines within a paragraph. Word wraps the lines for you; if you later add or remove text in the paragraph, Word adjusts the line breaks accordingly.

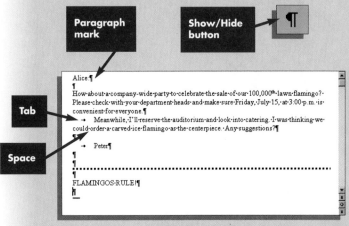

5 Click on the Show/Hide button in the Standard toolbar to see where you pressed the spacebar, Tab, and Enter keys. A dot represents a space, an arrow represents a tab, and a paragraph mark indicates where you pressed Enter. You can use the Show/Hide button to check whether you accidentally typed an extra space between two words (you'd see two dots instead of one) or to see how many blank lines you have between paragraphs. To turn Show/Hide off, just click on it again. You can delete extra spaces, tabs, and paragraph marks just as you'd delete regular characters.

TIP SHEET

▶ If you accidentally type the wrong character, press the Backspace key (the left-pointing arrow above the Enter key) to delete it. Do the same if you accidentally press Enter, Tab, or the spacebar. You'll learn other ways of correcting typing errors and revising your text in Chapter 5.

▶ The numeric keypad at the right end of your keyboard produces numbers only when your keyboard's number lock feature is active. Press the Num Lock key to turn number lock on and off. Of course, you can always type numbers using the number keys running across the top of your keyboard.

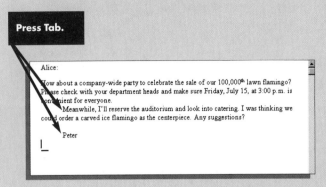

2 Press the Tab key to indent the first line of a paragraph. If you keep pressing Tab, you shift the line toward the right one-half inch at a time. To indent all the lines in the paragraph instead of just the first one, you need to use the indent feature (see Chapter 10).

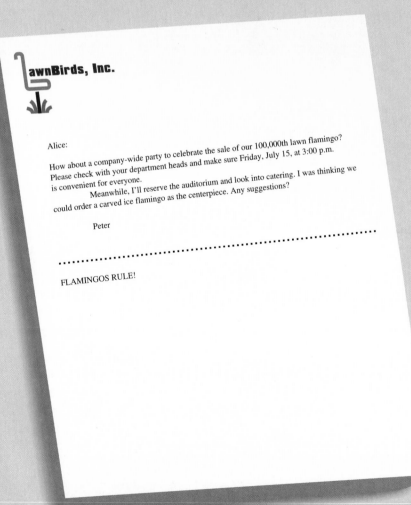

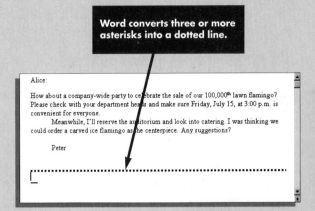

3 To type the same key repeatedly, hold the key down. Word automatically converts some repeated characters into different types of lines. For example, if you type three or more asterisks (*) and press Enter, Word replaces them with a dotted line, as shown here. Use the equal sign (=) for a double line, the tilde (~) for a wavy line, the pound (#) symbol for a thick decorative line, the hyphen (-) for a thin single line, or the underscore (_) for a thick single line.

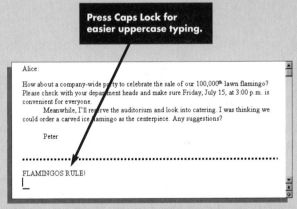

4 To produce all uppercase letters without having to hold down the Shift key, press the Caps Lock key once and then type. Press the Caps Lock key again when you're ready to switch off this feature. Caps Lock affects only the letter keys, not the number and punctuation keys. Thus, whether or not Caps Lock is on, you have to press Shift to type a character on the upper half of a number or punctuation key, such as * or %.

How to Save and Close a Document

A document you are typing exists only in your computer's memory, so if there's any chance that you'll want to come back to a document later, you should save it on a disk. The disk can be a floppy disk, a local hard disk, a network disk connected to your computer, or even a location on the Internet (see Chapter 20). After saving a document, you can continue working on it, or you can close it and move on to other work.

TIP SHEET

▶ **It's important to save a document soon after starting it and to resave it every few minutes as you change it, because if your computer loses power or otherwise malfunctions, you'll lose whatever is in memory. On disk, you will still have your document exactly as it was the last time you saved it.**

▶ **Anytime you open a document and make changes to it, but want to retain both the original document and the revised one, use the File, Save As command to save the revised document. Word displays the Save As dialog box to allow you to give the revised version a new name. Because you're saving it with a different name, it won't overwrite the original file on the disk.**

▶ **Word's AutoRecover feature periodically saves your document for you. However, you can't use AutoRecover as a substitute for saving the file yourself because the automatically saved file is deleted when you exit Word. This file is *only* used if your computer is shut off while Word is still in memory. When this happens, Word displays the automatically saved file for you the next time you start Word.**

▶ **Each drive on your computer system is assigned a letter. By convention, drive A is your floppy-disk drive, and drive C is your hard-disk drive. Any drives higher than C are other drives such as network drives, additional areas of your hard disk, or a CD-ROM drive.**

▶ **❶** As soon as you decide that the document you're typing is worth saving, click on the Save button in the Standard toolbar (or choose File, Save).

❾ If you continue working on your document, your changes won't be saved until you click on the Save button again. Since the document already has a name, no Save As dialog box appears when you issue the Save command. The revised document is saved, replacing the previous version.

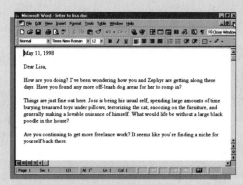

❽ Your document is now stored safely on disk, but a copy of it remains on the screen. Notice that the title bar contains the newly assigned file name. If you are done working on this document for now, close it by clicking on the Close button for the document window (the lower Close button), or choose File, Close.

2 The Save As dialog box appears because Word needs to know what to name the file and what folder to store it in. If you later revise this document and use the Save command to save it again, Word assumes you want to keep the same file name and location, so it automatically overwrites the original document on the disk with the revised one. If you want to keep both the original and revised versions of the document, use the File, Save As command instead (see the Tip Sheet).

3 Type a name for the document in the File Name text box. The file name can contain up to 255 characters, including spaces. The characters / \ > < * . ? " | : ; are not permitted in document names. Word automatically assigns the extension .doc to all Word documents, but this extension may not be visible on your computer. (To hide or display file name extensions, choose View, Options in any My Computer folder window or in the Windows Explorer, click on the View tab, mark or clear the check box labeled "Hide MS-DOS file extensions for file types that are registered," and click on OK.)

4 Observe the folder name in the box to the  right of Save In. This is the folder where the document will be stored if you don't specify otherwise. If this location is okay, skip the next two steps.

5 If the folder you want is a subfolder of the current folder (the one showing in the Save In box), double-click the folder name in the list. If the folder is contained in one of the subfolders, continue double-clicking on folder names until the one you want is showing in the Save In box. Then skip to step 7.

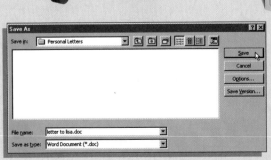

6 If the folder you want is not a subfolder of the current folder, click on the down arrow to the right of the Save In box, and click on the drive that contains the desired folder. Then double-click on folder names until the one you want is displayed in the Save In box.

 7 Click on the Save button to save the document under the specified name and in the specified folder.

How to Start a New Document

Sometimes you need to start a new document when you are in the middle of typing another one. You can start a new document even if you have not saved and closed the document you are currently working on. In fact, Word lets you have an unlimited number of documents open at the same time. If you have more than one document open, the active document is displayed on your screen, and the other open documents are hidden behind it. (See step 5 to find out how to switch among open documents.)

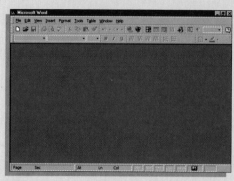

▶ **1** The Word window shown here appears when you have closed all your open documents. From here, you can either create a new document or open an existing document (see the next page).

TIP SHEET

▶ **When you use the New button to start a new document, Word automatically bases the new document on the Normal template. Every Word document is based on a *template*, which is like a blueprint for a document; the basic formatting (and sometimes text) is already in place for you. Word comes with well over 40 templates for everything from fax cover sheets to resumes to purchase orders. The Normal template is the one Word uses for standard documents. See Chapter 15 to learn how to use the other templates that come with Word.**

▶ **The fact that you can have more than one document open makes it easy to move and copy text from one document to another. Chapter 6 covers moving and copying text.**

▶ **It's a good idea to keep the number of documents open at the same time down to a minimum, since the more you have open, the slower your computer will run.**

2 Click on the New button on the Standard toolbar.

W Microsoft Word - Document2

3 Word creates a new document for you. The document's name in the title bar may be Document2, Document3, or even higher. As you start new documents throughout a work session, Word bumps up the number in this temporary name. When you save a document for the first time, the name you give it replaces the temporary name. The number in the name *does not* mean that you have that number of documents open. It just means you started that many documents in the current Word session (you may have already closed some of them).

4 After you create a new document, you can, if you like, keep it open while you create and/or open additional documents in the same Word session.

URGENT

Window Help
New Window
Arrange All
Split
✓ 1 Document2
2 letter to lisa.doc
3 permissions.doc
4 Rounds.doc
5 Waller St.doc

Five documents are currently open.

5 To switch among multiple open documents, click on Window in the menu bar, and then click on the desired document name in the lower part of the menu.

How to Open a Document from Disk

The benefit of saving a document on disk is that you can later open (redisplay) it for revision or reprinting. You can follow the steps on this page to open a document on your hard disk, a floppy disk, a network drive, or a location on the Internet (see Chapter 20). Starting in Chapter 5, you'll learn about the many ways to edit a document once it's open.

1 Click on the Open button in the Standard toolbar to display the Open dialog box (or choose File, Open).

TIP SHEET

▶ **Whenever you want to create a new document that will be similar to one you already have on disk, you can save yourself some typing by opening the original document, making changes to it, and then saving the revised version under a new name. That way, you'll still have the original document on disk along with the new one. After opening the document, choose File, Save As. Specify a name and location for the revised version (see "How to Save and Close a Document" at the beginning of this chapter) and click on the Save button.**

▶ **Word offers a convenient way to open one of the last four documents you worked on. Display the File menu and notice the document names at the bottom of the menu. If the document you want to open appears on the list, simply click on it.**

▶ **From the Open dialog box, you can also print, move, copy, delete, or rename a file. Point to the file name and click the right mouse button to display a context menu, then click on the desired command.**

8 A copy of the document is displayed on your screen (the original document is still on the disk). You are now free to change and/or print the document. If you do make changes, be sure to save the document to update the copy on disk. If you don't make any changes (or if you make changes you don't like), you can close the document without saving it—this preserves the document on disk in its original form.

7 Locate the document you want to open, and double-click on it (or click on it once and then click on the Open button).

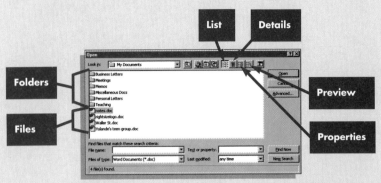

2 Note the List, Details, Properties, and Preview buttons. You can use these buttons to change the way your folders and files are displayed in the dialog box. For now, click on the List button to display the folders and files in a simple list. Feel free to experiment with the other three buttons to see how they change your display.

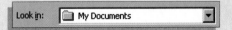

3 Observe the entry in the Look In box. It tells you what location is currently being displayed. If the document you want to open is in this location, skip the next two steps.

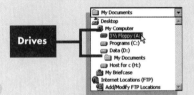

4 If your document is located somewhere else, click on the arrow to the right of the Look In box, locate the disk drive containing the document, and click on it. For example, if the document is on a floppy disk, click on 3½ Floppy (A:).

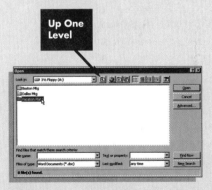

6 Word shows you every document in the specified location whose name ends with the extension .doc. If the document you need does not have a .doc extension, display the Files of Type list and then click on All Files (*.*). Now you'll see all the documents stored in the specified location.

5 All of the folders and files in the drive you clicked on are displayed in the dialog box. Locate the folder that contains your document—use the scroll bar if necessary—and double-click on it. To see the folders inside of any folder, double-click on the folder name. To move back up to the folder that contains the one you're currently viewing, click on the Up One Level button.

CHAPTER 2

Printing

Printing is what word processing is all about. Unless you're creating a document that you intend to publish at a Web site or otherwise distribute electronically (see Chapter 20), the printed page is all your readers will see. Though crucial, printing in Word is not a hassle; Word's printing options are straightforward and easy to use.

Windows tells Word what printer is attached to your computer and what it can do, and then it works behind the scenes to feed your documents to the printer. You just turn your printer on, issue a command in Word, and collect your document at the printer.

Nevertheless, there are a few printing-related options you need to know about. This chapter explains how to preview your document before printing, how to print an entire document, how to print specific portions of a document, and how to print multiple copies.

How to Preview a Document Before Printing

Word lets you see what the printed document will look like before you actually send it to the printer. Using Print Preview is a great way to avoid wasting paper, because you can spot problems in your document before you print, not after. For example, you many discover that your page numbers aren't displaying correctly (see Chapter 12 to learn how to insert page numbers) or that you have too much blank space between two sections of a report.

▶ **1** Click on the Print Preview button in the Standard toolbar (or choose File, Print Preview).

7 To close Print Preview, click on the Close button in the middle of the Print Preview toolbar.

TIP SHEET

▶ **If your document is spilling over onto two pages and you'd like to get it to fit on one page, you can use the Shrink to Fit button in the Print Preview toolbar. Shrink to Fit adjusts your margins and possibly the font size to make the text fit on a single page.**

▶ **You can print directly from the Print Preview screen. Either click on the Print button in the Print Preview toolbar or choose File, Print.**

▶ **You can edit your text when you are viewing it in Print Preview. Just magnify the page so that the text is legible, turn off the Magnifier button, click to place an insertion point on the page, and edit as you normally do.**

▶ **The keyboard shortcut to switch to Print Preview is Ctrl + F2.**

Print Preview toolbar

3 Press the Page Up and Page Down keys to view your document page by page.

2 Notice that [Preview] is added to the title bar, and the Print Preview toolbar is now displayed at the top of your screen.

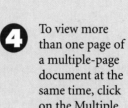

Drag to select the number of pages.

4 To view more than one page of a multiple-page document at the same time, click on the Multiple Pages button in the Print Preview toolbar. A grid drops down with small squares that represent pages. Drag through the desired number of squares to highlight them. For example, to view four pages, drag through four squares. (The grid enlarges as you drag.)

Magnifier

One Page

Multiple Pages

Shrink to Fit

Click here to close Print Preview.

Print

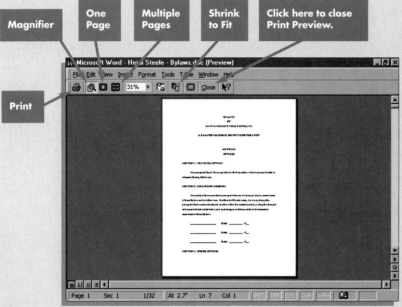

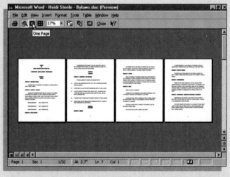

5 To view just one page again, click on the One Page button.

6 If you want to magnify a particular portion of a page, click on the Magnifier button in the Print Preview toolbar (if it is not already selected). When you point to the page, the mouse pointer becomes a magnifying glass with a plus sign. (If you are viewing multiple pages, you have to click once on the page you want to magnify before the mouse pointer changes to a magnifying glass.) Click on the portion of the page you want to magnify. The area you clicked on enlarges, and the plus sign in the mouse pointer changes to a minus sign. To view the full page again, click on the page once more.

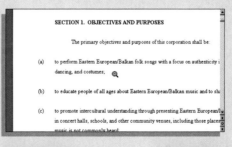

How to Print a Document

Word assumes that you will frequently want to print one complete copy of the document on your screen, so it provides a toolbar button to let you do just that. With a couple of extra steps, you can also customize your printing in a variety of ways. Maybe you need to show a paragraph or two of your proposal to a coworker, or maybe you made a minor correction on only one page of a long report.

Word for Windows makes it easy to print the current page, a range of pages, or a more specific portion such as a sentence or a paragraph. You can also print multiple copies of your document, which comes in handy when the copier is on the fritz.

TIP SHEET

▸ **To use a printer other than the one listed at the top of the Print dialog box, click the down arrow to the right of the printer name to display a list of installed printers, then click on the one you want.**

▸ **You can easily check which printer is currently selected without displaying the Print dialog box. Just point to the Print toolbar button—the ScreenTip includes the name of the selected printer.**

▸ **The keyboard shortcut for displaying the Print dialog box is Ctrl+P.**

▸ **Click the Properties button to adjust various settings for the currently selected printer.**

▸ **In step 6, you don't need to click on the Pages option button. As soon as you type page numbers in the Pages text box, Word selects the Pages button automatically.**

▶ **1** To print one copy of the entire document, make sure your printer is turned on and has paper, and click on the Print button in the Standard toolbar. That's all there is to it—Word sends the document to your printer without asking you any questions at all. If you want to customize your printing, follow the remaining steps on this page.

8 After you've made your selections, click on the OK button to print. If you decide not to print, make sure to use the Cancel button to close the Print dialog box without issuing a command.

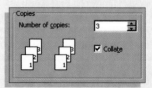

 7 To print more than one copy of your document, type the desired number in the Number of Copies text box. (You can also change the number by clicking the increment arrows.)

② To print the current page, click on that page to place your insertion point there. If you want to print a small block of text, select it by dragging over it with the mouse. (You'll learn other ways to select text in Chapter 5.)

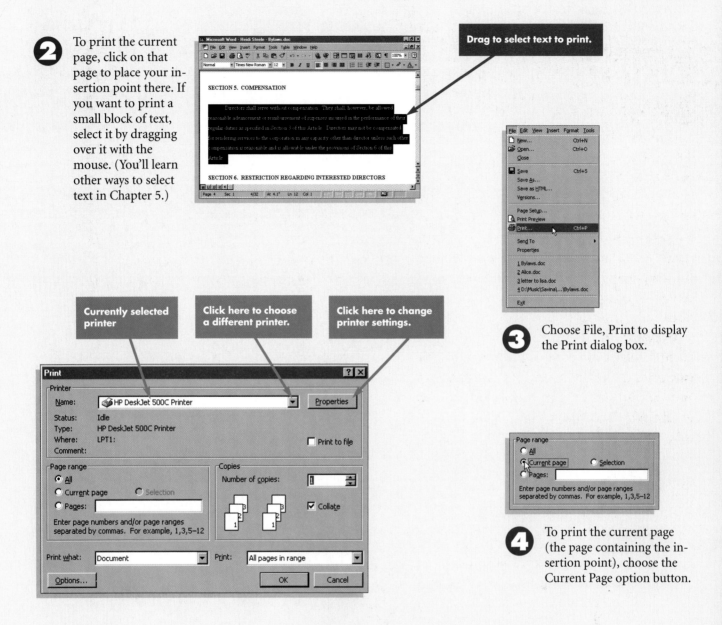

Drag to select text to print.

③ Choose File, Print to display the Print dialog box.

Currently selected printer

Click here to choose a different printer.

Click here to change printer settings.

④ To print the current page (the page containing the insertion point), choose the Current Page option button.

⑥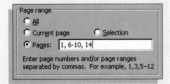

To print a range of pages, click in the Pages text box and type the page range. Use a hyphen to indicate a contiguous range of pages, and use commas to separate noncontiguous pages. In this example, Word will print pages 1, 6 through 10, and 14.

⑤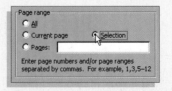

If you selected text in step 2 and you want to print only that block of text, choose the Selection option button. (This option button is only active when you have selected text.)

CHAPTER 3

Help and Rescue

A crucial part of becoming self-sufficient in a powerful program such as Word is learning how to bail yourself out when you run into trouble. By making full use of the tools described in this chapter—the Office Assistant, online help, and Undo—you'll be able to solve most problems yourself, instead of relying on the computer guru at your office or your computer-savvy kids.

The Office Assistant, available in all Microsoft Office 97 programs, makes it quick and painless to broaden your knowledge of Word as you work. Displayed on screen as an animated character (you can choose among several), the Office Assistant watches how you are doing things and helps you incorporate new techniques "on the fly."

If talking to an animated paper clip or bouncing ball is not your style, you can always get help the old-fashioned way: by consulting Word's online help system directly. In this chapter, you learn how to use the help system's table of contents and index to find the exact information you're looking for.

Finally, if you make a mistake, whether it's issuing the wrong command or deleting some text by accident, you can probably undo it with Word's Undo command. Word keeps track of all your recent actions. Even if you don't notice a mistake until you've made several more revisions to your document, you can still fix the problem by reversing all your actions back to, and including, the mistake.

How to Use the Office Assistant

Thoughtful, friendly, and well informed, the Office Assistant handles everything short of reminding you to take breaks and fixing you cappuccinos. In addition to offering tips on how to type and format your documents more efficiently, the Office Assistant helps you search Word's online help system, offers timely assistance with many tasks, and provides alerts about events that require your attention, all with amusing sound effects (assuming your computer has a sound card) and animation. Even if "cute" is usually not your style, you might want to give the Office Assistant a try—you'll probably find it useful in spite of yourself.

TIP SHEET

▶ **You can change the way the Office Assistant behaves to suit your preferences. Right-click on the Office Assistant window, and click on Options to display the Options tab of the Office Assistant dialog box. Mark or clear the check boxes for the various options, and click on OK.**

▶ **The default Office Assistant is a paper clip figure named *Clippit*. If you want to use one of the other eight assistants, such as the puppy shown on this page (named *Power Pup*), right-click on the Office Assistant window and select Choose Assistant from the context menu. Word displays Office Assistant dialog box with the Gallery tab in front. Use the Next and Back buttons to check out the other assistants. When you find one you want to try, click on OK.**

▶ **Depending on your installation of Word, you may not have all the Office Assistants installed. If you try to change the assistant as described in the preceding tip and see a message stating that the Assistant file can't be located, insert the Office 97 CD to let Word copy the necessary files.**

▶ **1** If the Office Assistant isn't currently displayed, click on the Office Assistant button at the right end of the Standard toolbar. (You can hide the Office Assistant at any time by clicking the toolbar button again, or by clicking the Close button in the Office Assistant window.)

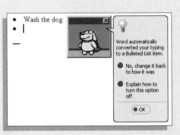

8 The Office Assistant also alerts you the first time Word applies certain types of automatic formatting. In this example, when the user typed * *Wash the dog* and pressed Enter, Word converted the asterisk to a bullet and applied the bullet list format. Office Assistant explains the change, and lets you reverse it or find out how to turn off the feature.

7 As you're working in Word, the Office Assistant observes your actions and offers assistance that relates to what you're doing. In this example, the Office Assistant recognized the text as the beginning of a letter, and offered help with completing it.

2 The Office Assistant watches the tasks you perform, and when it has a tip on how you could do something more efficiently, it displays a light bulb in the Office Assistant window. Click on the light bulb to display the tip. (If the Office Assistant is not currently displayed, you can still tell when a tip is waiting because the Office Assistant toolbar button displays a light bulb as well.)

3 The Office Assistant offers the tip shown here if you issue the Find command the "long way," by choosing Edit, Find. (You'll learn about the Find feature in Chapter 5.) Click on the Close button to hide the tip.

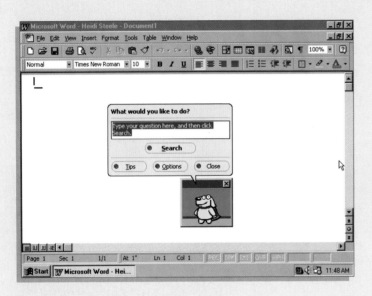

4 If you want the Office Assistant to search the online help system for a particular topic, click anywhere in the Office Assistant window (or press F1) to display the yellow box shown here. Type the name of the topic you want help with, and click on the Search button. In this case, the Office Assistant will look through the help system for information about working with envelopes.

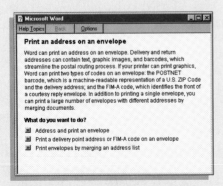

6 The Office Assistant displays the information from the help system.

5 If the Office Assistant finds several topics that relate to the search text, it displays a list of choices. Click on a topic of interest.

How to Use the Help Contents and Index

Word's online help system covers everything from simple tasks, such as how to delete text or save a document, to detailed reference information that only programmers need to know. While the Office Assistant provides the speediest access to help, you might at times want to investigate a topic in depth by delving into the help system directly. This page describes how to look up information via the help system's table of contents and index.

▶ ❶ Choose Help, Contents and Index to display the Help Topics: Microsoft Word dialog box.

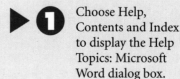

❽ Word displays the topic. You can click on the Help Topics button to return to the main Help Topics: Microsoft Word dialog box. When you're ready to leave the help system, simply click on the Close button in the upper-right corner of the help dialog box you're currently viewing.

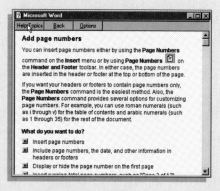

❼ In many cases, Word displays the Topics Found dialog box to let you choose among several topics related to the term you selected in the previous step. Double-click on the topic you want to read about.

❻ The index is often the fastest way of finding information. To use it, click on the Index tab, and type the first few letters of the word or phrase you're looking for. When you begin typing, Word scrolls the alphabetical list to display terms beginning with the letters you typed. When you see a topic that interests you, double-click on it.

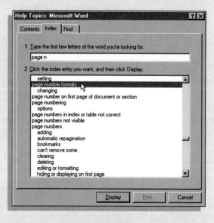

TIP SHEET

▶ To print a help topic, click on the Options button at the top of the dialog box (see steps 4 and 8), choose the Print Topics command, and click on OK in the Print dialog box.

▶ In addition to the Contents and Index tabs, the Help Topics: Microsoft Word dialog box includes a third tab called Find. Find lets you search for all help topics whose contents contain the word you specify. This is useful if you're not sure how a topic would be categorized in the table of contents or index, but you have some idea what words are likely to appear in the text of the topic.

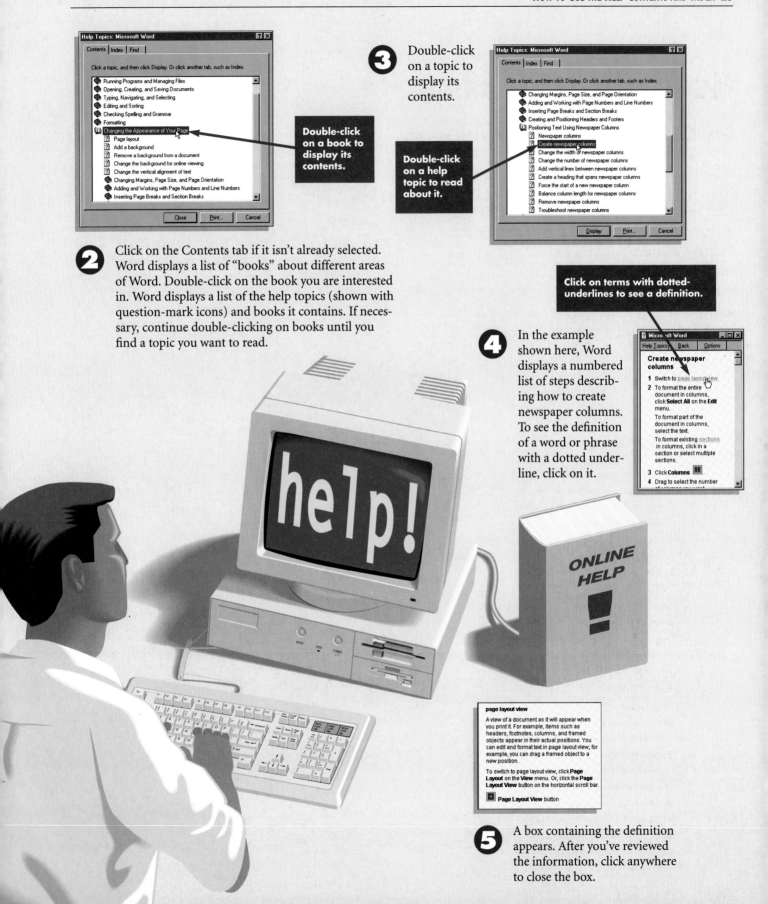

3 Double-click on a topic to display its contents.

Double-click on a book to display its contents.

Double-click on a help topic to read about it.

Click on terms with dotted-underlines to see a definition.

2 Click on the Contents tab if it isn't already selected. Word displays a list of "books" about different areas of Word. Double-click on the book you are interested in. Word displays a list of the help topics (shown with question-mark icons) and books it contains. If necessary, continue double-clicking on books until you find a topic you want to read.

4 In the example shown here, Word displays a numbered list of steps describing how to create newspaper columns. To see the definition of a word or phrase with a dotted underline, click on it.

5 A box containing the definition appears. After you've reviewed the information, click anywhere to close the box.

How to Undo Actions

Word lets you undo most actions, including typing, deleting (thank goodness), moving and copying, and formatting text. You'll find out how to do all these things in the upcoming chapters, but it's a good idea to learn how to undo them first! One of the best aspects of Word's Undo feature is that it lets you undo multiple actions, not just your most recent one. As you experiment with Undo, keep in mind that Word cannot undo certain actions, such as opening, saving, or printing a document.

Click here to undo your most recent action.

► **1** The Undo button in the Standard toolbar is composed of two parts: the button itself, and a down arrow to its right.

TIP SHEET

▶ **In addition to using the Undo toolbar button, you can issue the Undo command by choosing Edit, Undo, or by pressing Ctrl+Z.**

▶ **When you're working in a dialog box, you can revoke your selections right away by pressing the Escape (Esc) key or clicking on Cancel to close the dialog box without issuing a command. If you've already closed a dialog box by clicking on the OK button, then you have to use Undo to reverse the command.**

▶ **If you open a document from disk, make several revisions, and then decide you don't like the changes you've made, you don't have to undo every change. Instead, simply close the document, and when Word asks if you want to save your changes, click on the No button. The original copy of the document will remain on disk in its unrevised state.**

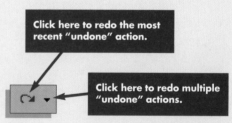

Click here to redo the most recent "undone" action.

Click here to redo multiple "undone" actions.

7 If the Undo command did not produce the result you expected, you can use the Redo button (just to the right of Undo in the Standard toolbar) to reverse the undo. Click on the Redo button one or more times to redo actions one by one. Optionally, you can click on the down arrow to the right of the Redo button to display a list of "undone" actions, and click on one of them to redo everything back to that point.

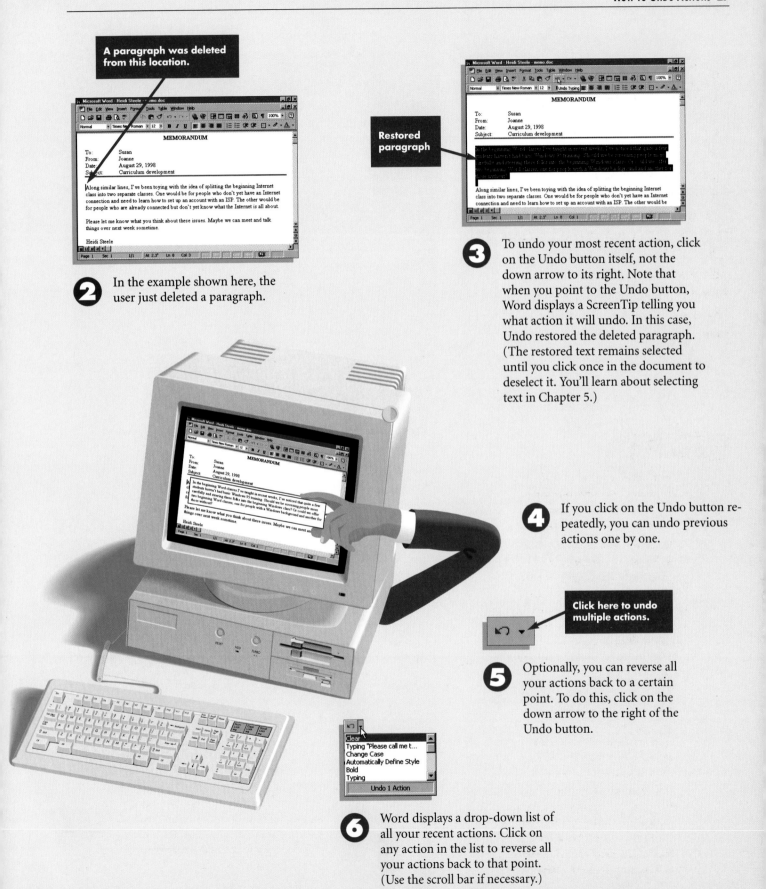

A paragraph was deleted from this location.

Restored paragraph

2 In the example shown here, the user just deleted a paragraph.

3 To undo your most recent action, click on the Undo button itself, not the down arrow to its right. Note that when you point to the Undo button, Word displays a ScreenTip telling you what action it will undo. In this case, Undo restored the deleted paragraph. (The restored text remains selected until you click once in the document to deselect it. You'll learn about selecting text in Chapter 5.)

4 If you click on the Undo button repeatedly, you can undo previous actions one by one.

Click here to undo multiple actions.

5 Optionally, you can reverse all your actions back to a certain point. To do this, click on the down arrow to the right of the Undo button.

6 Word displays a drop-down list of all your recent actions. Click on any action in the list to reverse all your actions back to that point. (Use the scroll bar if necessary.)

CHAPTER 4

Changing the Display

Word offers a wide assortment of options for changing the appearance of the Word window. If you only type letters and memos, you may not need to adjust any of the default settings. However, if you create specialized types of documents, or if you spend a lot of time word processing, you may want to tailor Word's appearance to suit your own preferences.

This chapter begins with an explanation of how to change the *view* of your document. The default view, *Normal view*, doesn't display the margins of the page. If you want to see text in the margin areas, you have to switch to *Page Layout view. Full Screen view* gives you more room to work by hiding everything on your screen but your document.

Next, you learn how to change the magnification of the document. While Word normally displays text at approximately the size it will be when printed, you may at times—such as when you're working with especially small or large font sizes—need to enlarge or shrink the text on the screen to make it easier to read and edit.

The third topic explains how to *split* the document window. This feature is extremely useful if you create long documents, because it lets you view two separate sections of a document at the same time.

Finally, you learn how to customize your toolbars. You learn how to display and hide toolbars, how to move them around the Word window, and how to change which buttons they contain.

How to Change Views

Word assumes you want to use Normal view. This view is fine most of the time, but it doesn't show you the margin areas of your document. If you want to see text you've typed into the margins—such as headers, footers, and page numbers—you need to switch to *Page Layout view*. (A *header* is a block of text that prints in the top margin of each page; a *footer* prints in the bottom margin. You'll learn how to add headers and footers in Chapter 12.) You also need to use Page Layout view to work with newspaper-style columns and graphics. *Full Screen view* clears everything off your screen but your document, thus letting you see more of your text. You can edit your document in any of the views.

1 Click on View in the menu bar and confirm that you're currently using Normal view (the button next to the command should look like it's pushed in). If you aren't in Normal view, switch to it now by clicking on Normal.

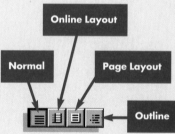

8 A fast way of switching between Normal and Page Layout views is to use the view buttons in the lower-left corner of your screen. (See the Tip Sheet for a brief description of Outline view and Online Layout view.)

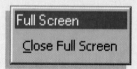

7 To close Full Screen view, click on the Close Full Screen command in the small Full Screen toolbar.

② The margin areas aren't visible in Normal view; if your document is more than one page long, Word uses horizontal dotted lines to indicate page breaks (more about page breaks in Chapter 11).

③ Choose View, Page Layout to switch to Page Layout view.

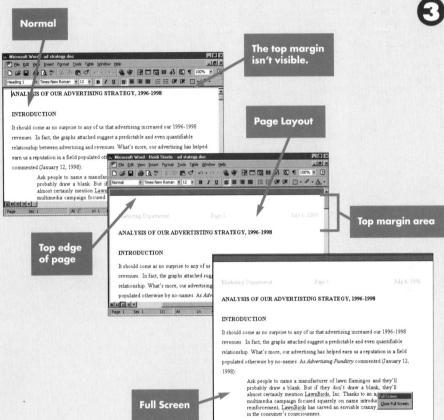

Normal

The top margin isn't visible.

Page Layout

Top edge of page

Top margin area

Full Screen

④ In Page Layout view, the margin areas are visible, so you can see the document's header and footer text (although the header text is dim in this example because the header and footer areas are not currently active). Page breaks show as actual separations between on-screen "pages" of text.

⑤ Click on the View menu again, and this time click on Full Screen to switch to Full Screen view.

⑥ In Full Screen view, Word hides the title bar, menu bar, toolbars, and so on to give you a large, uncluttered view of your document. If you switch to Full Screen view from Page Layout view, as described here, the margin areas will be displayed. If you switch from Normal view, the margin areas will be hidden.

How to Zoom In and Out

If your document has very small text, you might need to *zoom in* on it (enlarge it) to make the text easier to edit. On the other hand, if you're working with large text, or you're laying out a flyer or a résumé, you might need to *zoom out* (shrink the document) so that you can see more of the document at one time. Changing the zoom setting does not affect how the document will print, only how it appears on the screen.

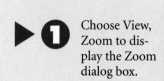 ▶ **1** Choose View, Zoom to display the Zoom dialog box.

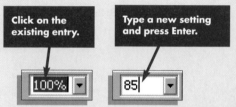

Click on the existing entry.

Type a new setting and press Enter.

6 If the zoom setting you want is not one of the options in the list, you can type it directly into the Zoom Control box. Click on the current entry to select it, and then type the desired percentage; it will replace the selected entry. Then press Enter to apply the new setting.

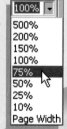

5 Click on the desired setting. The options in this list change depending on which view you are using.

TIP SHEET

▶ **Any zoom setting above 100% (such as 150% or 200%) magnifies the document so that you can see less of it on your screen. Any setting under 100% (such as 75% or 50%) shrinks the document so that you can see more of it on your screen.**

▶ **The Page Width setting magnifies or shrinks your document just enough so that it will fit across the width of your screen.**

These options are not available in Normal view.

2 Click on the desired zoom setting. Word shows you a sample of the setting in the Preview area. The Whole Page and Many Pages options are only available if you're using Page Layout view. (In Page Layout view, you can click on the Many Pages button to display a grid of squares representing pages, and then drag across the number of pages you want to see.) Click on OK to close the dialog box.

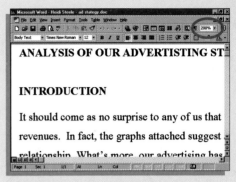

3 Word applies the zoom setting you chose.

Click here to display list of zoom settings.

4 As an alternative to using the Zoom dialog box, you can change the zoom setting via the Zoom Control box at the right end of the Standard toolbar. Click on the down arrow to display a list of settings.

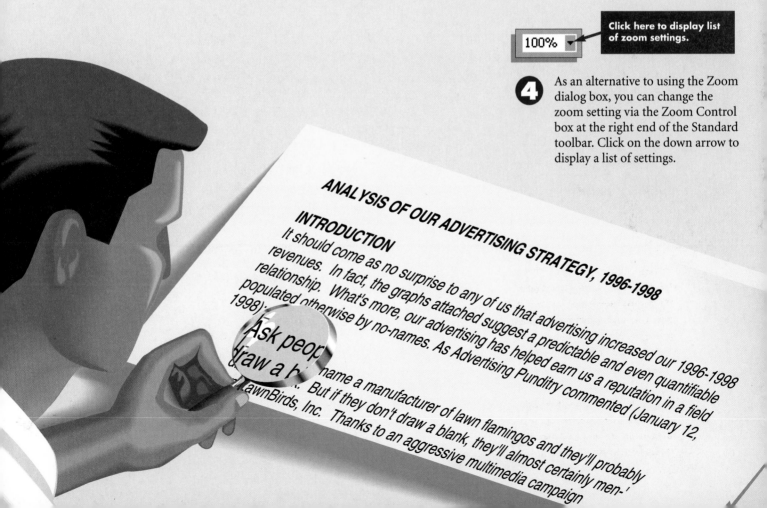

How to Split the Screen

When you're working with a long document, you may occasionally want to display two sections of the document that are separated by several pages of text. For example, if a report contains a set of figures, you may want to refer to those figures even as you're typing in some other part of the report. You view two separate parts of a long document by splitting the screen into two panes and then scrolling each pane independently.

Position the mouse pointer over the split bar.

▶ **1** Move your mouse pointer over the *split bar*, the short gray horizontal line just above the vertical scroll bar. The mouse pointer changes shape to display two black arrows.

5 To adjust the position of the split, place your mouse pointer anywhere on the split (you'll see the *Resize* ScreenTip) and drag it to a new location. To remove the split, place the mouse pointer over the split and double-click.

Resize

2 Drag down the vertical scroll bar. As you drag, a gray line running across the screen indicates where the window will be split if you release the mouse button. Release the mouse button when the line is about midway down the window.

Drag to create a split.

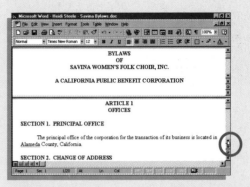

3 Your document window is split into two panes. Notice that you have a separate vertical scroll bar for each pane. Try using both scroll bars—you can scroll through each pane independently to bring different portions of the same document into view.

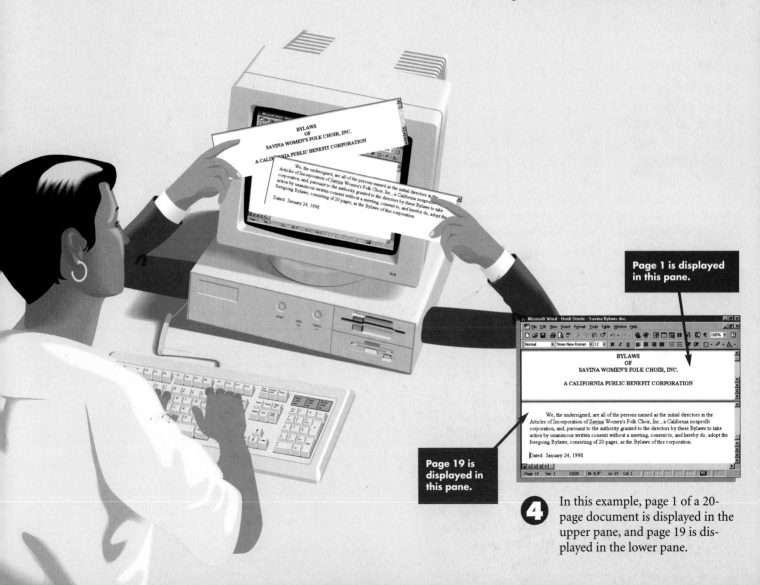

Page 1 is displayed in this pane.

Page 19 is displayed in this pane.

4 In this example, page 1 of a 20-page document is displayed in the upper pane, and page 19 is displayed in the lower pane.

How to Customize the Toolbars

In addition to the Standard and Formatting toolbars, Word offers many other toolbars you can use for particular types of tasks. For instance, if you and several other people are collaborating on a document, you might want to display the Reviewing toolbar, which contains buttons that let you keep track of who made what changes to a document. You can also hide toolbars you don't use frequently to free up space on your screen. Word lets you position toolbars anywhere you like in the Word window, and you can also customize the toolbars themselves, by deleting buttons, moving them to new positions, or copying them from one toolbar to another.

TIP SHEET

▶ **You can display (or hide) the Drawing and Web toolbars by simply clicking on the Drawing and Web Toolbar buttons on the Standard toolbar.**

▶ **If you modify the buttons on a toolbar and then wish you hadn't, you can change the toolbar back to the form it was in when Word was installed. To do this, choose Tools, Customize to display the Customize dialog box. Click on the Toolbars tab, click on the toolbar in question, click on the Reset button, and then click on OK. Finally, click on the Close button in the Customize dialog box.**

▶ **If a command you use frequently doesn't have a button on the toolbars you use, you can easily add one. Choose Tools, Customize to display the Customize dialog box, click on the Commands tab, and browse through the Categories list to display groups of related commands in the Commands list. When you find the one you want, drag it out of the dialog box and onto the desired toolbar. Release the mouse, and click on the Close button in the Customize dialog box.**

▶ **1** To use a toolbar that's currently hidden, choose View, Toolbars, to display the Toolbars submenu. The currently displayed toolbars have check marks next to their names (the Standard and Formatting toolbars in this example). Click on the toolbar you want to display.

Position the black I-beam and release the mouse. **Button to be copied**

8 To copy a button to a different toolbar (leaving it in its original location), hold down the Alt key and the Ctrl key as you drag the button to the desired location. Word adds a plus sign to the mouse pointer to indicate that you are copying, not moving, the button. When the black I-beam is in the right position, release the Alt key and the mouse first, and then release the Ctrl key. Here, the Columns button is being copied from the Standard toolbar to the Formatting toolbar.

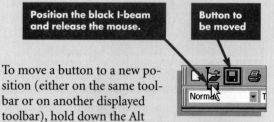

Position the black I-beam and release the mouse. **Button to be moved**

7 To move a button to a new position (either on the same toolbar or on another displayed toolbar), hold down the Alt key as you drag the button to the new location. A large black I-beam indicates where the button will be placed when you release the mouse. In this example, the Save button is being moved to the left side of the Open button.

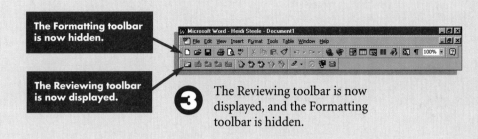

The Formatting toolbar is now hidden.

The Reviewing toolbar is now displayed.

3 The Reviewing toolbar is now displayed, and the Formatting toolbar is hidden.

2 To hide a toolbar, choose View, Toolbars, and click on the toolbar you want to hide.

Drag the toolbar to a new location.

4 To move a toolbar to a different part of the Word window, point to the vertical double line at the far left edge of the toolbar, and drag the toolbar to the new location. If you release the mouse while the toolbar is in the middle of the window, the toolbar will "float" over the text area. You can also drag the toolbar to an edge of the window and release the mouse to "dock" the toolbar.

The toolbar is docked at the bottom of the screen.

5 In this example, the Reviewing toolbar is now docked at the bottom of the screen.

6 To remove a button from a toolbar, hold down the Alt key as you drag the button from the toolbar into the text area, and release the mouse. As you drag, Word attaches a button icon to the mouse pointer; when the pointer is over the text area, it adds an X to the pointer to indicate that the button will be deleted. Here, the Format Painter button is being deleted from the Standard toolbar.

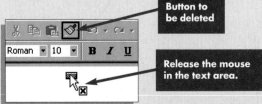

Button to be deleted

Release the mouse in the text area.

CHAPTER 5

Editing Fundamentals

The process of editing can range from fixing the occasional typo to rewriting sentences or reworking entire paragraphs. Regardless of the extent of your revisions, the mechanics of editing in Word are straightforward and easy to master, letting you concentrate on the writing itself.

This is the first of four chapters devoted to editing; the skills you learn here provide a foundation for the editing techniques introduced in Chapters 6 through 8.

The first two topics teach you different ways of navigating through a document. You learn many keyboard and mouse shortcuts for moving quickly from one place to another, and you find out about *browse* and *go to*, two features that let you jump to particular objects in a document, including pages, graphics, and headings.

The last three topics explain essential techniques for editing in any document. You learn how to insert text into passages you've already typed, how to *select* (highlight) text in preparation for performing an action on it, and how to delete text.

As a side note, you may see Word's AutoCorrect feature at work as you edit your documents. AutoCorrect makes some editing changes automatically. For example, it changes *adn*, a common misspelling, to *and*, and it replaces *(c)* with the copyright symbol ©. You'll learn more about AutoCorrect in Chapter 7.

How to Navigate in a Document

Before you can do any editing in your document, you need to know how to *navigate*—how to move the insertion point to the position where you want to edit the text. While you can move through an entire document using only the four arrow keys, this gets cumbersome and time consuming if your document is more than a few pages long. Word provides several useful keyboard shortcuts for moving longer distances, and it is worth your while to spend a bit of time practicing them so they become second nature.

TIP SHEET

▶ **To use the mouse to move the insertion point to a part of your document that's currently showing on screen, just point to the desired location and click once.**

▶ **To use the mouse to move the insertion point to a part of your document that isn't currently visible, use the vertical scroll bar on the right side of the Word window. If you drag the scroll box on the bar, Word shows you the page number you will jump to if you release the mouse. After you've scrolled to a new location, click once to move the insertion point before you start typing.**

▶ **As you navigate through a multiple-page document, you'll periodically see single dotted lines running across the page. These are *automatic page breaks*. Word calculates how many lines can fit on each page, and begins new pages for you. To force a page to break before it is full, you have to insert a *manual page break*. You'll learn how to do that in Chapter 11.**

▶ **1** The steps on this page involve using the keyboard to navigate. See the Tip Sheet for help on moving the insertion point with the mouse. You'll normally use some combination of keyboard and mouse techniques to navigate through your documents.

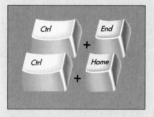

8 Press Ctrl+End to move the insertion point to the end of the document and Ctrl+Home to move to the beginning of the document.

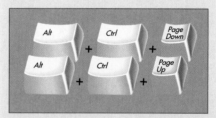

7 Press Alt+Ctrl+PgDn to move the insertion point down to the top of the next page and Alt+Ctrl+PgUp to move to the top of the previous page. You can also use the browse feature to jump from page to page, as described on the next page.

6 Press PgDn to move the insertion point down one screen at a time and PgUp to move up one screen at a time.

2 Press the → and ← arrows to move to the right and left one character at a time. Press the ↑ and ↓ arrows to move up and down one line at a time. If you press and hold down any of the arrow keys, you will scroll quickly in the direction of the arrow. This technique is fast, but it's also hard to control. At the most rudimentary level, the four arrow keys are all you need to navigate through a document of any length.

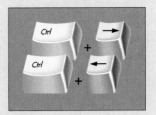

3 Press Ctrl+→ to move the insertion point to the right one word at a time and Ctrl+← to move to the left one word at a time.

4 Press Ctrl+↓ to move the insertion point down one paragraph at a time and Ctrl+↑ to move up one paragraph at a time. Note that Word stops on blank lines and short lines of text as well as on longer paragraphs. Word considers any text followed by a paragraph mark to be a paragraph. (A paragraph mark gets inserted wherever you press Enter.) Since blank lines and short lines of text end with paragraph marks, Word treats them as individual paragraphs.

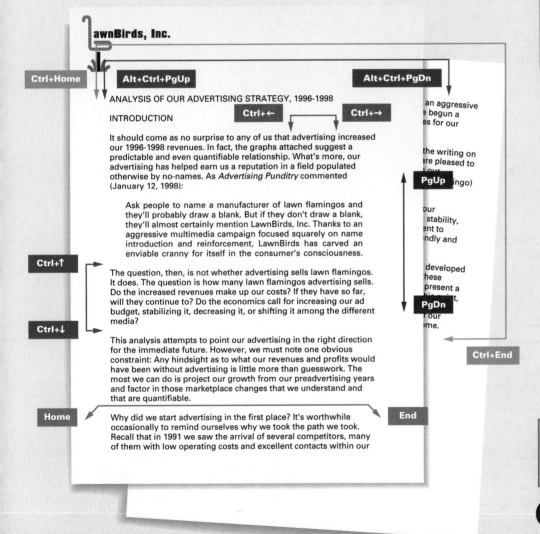

LawnBirds, Inc.

Ctrl+Home

Alt+Ctrl+PgUp   **Alt+Ctrl+PgDn**

ANALYSIS OF OUR ADVERTISING STRATEGY, 1996-1998

INTRODUCTION

Ctrl+←   **Ctrl+→**

It should come as no surprise to any of us that advertising increased our 1996-1998 revenues. In fact, the graphs attached suggest a predictable and even quantifiable relationship. What's more, our advertising has helped earn us a reputation in a field populated otherwise by no-names. As *Advertising Punditry* commented (January 12, 1998):

> Ask people to name a manufacturer of lawn flamingos and they'll probably draw a blank. But if they don't draw a blank, they'll almost certainly mention LawnBirds, Inc. Thanks to an aggressive multimedia campaign focused squarely on name introduction and reinforcement, LawnBirds has carved an enviable cranny for itself in the consumer's consciousness.

Ctrl+↑

The question, then, is not whether advertising sells lawn flamingos. It does. The question is how many lawn flamingos advertising sells. Do the increased revenues make up our costs? If they have so far, will they continue to? Do the economics call for increasing our ad budget, stabilizing it, decreasing it, or shifting it among the different media?

Ctrl+↓

This analysis attempts to point our advertising in the right direction for the immediate future. However, we must note one obvious constraint: Any hindsight as to what our revenues and profits would have been without advertising is little more than guesswork. The most we can do is project our growth from our preadvertising years and factor in those marketplace changes that we understand and that are quantifiable.

Home   **End**

Why did we start advertising in the first place? It's worthwhile occasionally to remind ourselves why we took the path we took. Recall that in 1991 we saw the arrival of several competitors, many of them with low operating costs and excellent contacts within our

an aggressive
e begun a
es for our

the writing on
re pleased to

PgUp ingo)

our
stability,
ent to
ndly and

developed
hese
present a
int,
our
me.

PgDn

Ctrl+End

5 Press Home to move the insertion point to the beginning of the line you're on, and press End to move to the end of the line.

How to Use Browse and Go To

Browsing (see steps 1 through 6) is a fast way to move sequentially through your document. You can use several types of objects as the focus point for browsing—including pages, headings, graphics, and footnotes—and you can change the browse object at any time. Go To (see steps 7 and 8) lets you move nonsequentially to an object of your choosing. For example, you can use the Go To command to jump directly to a particular page in a long document.

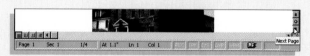

1 Point to the Next and Previous arrows. The default option is to browse by page, so the buttons are labeled Next Page and Previous Page. Notice the page you're currently on (page 1 in this example) and click on the Next Page button.

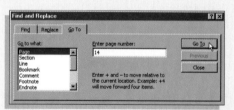

8 Word displays the Find and Replace dialog box with the Go To tab in front. In the Go To What list, select the type of object you want to go to (the default choice is Page). Next, use the box in the middle of the dialog box to specify the exact object. Because Page is selected in this example, the box is labeled Enter Page Number. Finally, click on the Go To button or press Enter to jump to the object. When you're done using Go To, click on the Close button.

7 To use Go To, double-click anywhere along the left two-thirds of the status bar. (You can also choose Edit, Go To, or click on the Go To object in the Select Browse Object grid shown in step 4.)

TIP SHEET

► **The keyboard equivalent of clicking on the Next Page and Previous Page buttons (see step 1) is to press Alt+Ctrl+PgDn and Alt+Ctrl+PgUp.**

► **In addition to the Go To tab described in step 8, the Find and Replace dialog box contains tabs for Find and Replace. You learn how to use these tabs in Chapter 6.**

► **The Find and Replace dialog box is unusual in that it allows you to edit your document while the dialog box is displayed. If you see something that needs to be revised while the dialog box is open, just click in the document and make the desired changes. When you're finished, click the title bar of the dialog box to activate it again.**

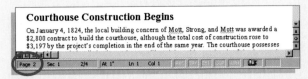

Courthouse Construction Begins

On January 4, 1824, the local building concern of Mott, Strong, and Mott was awarded a $2,800 contract to build the courthouse, although the total cost of construction rose to $3,197 by the project's completion in the end of the same year. The courthouse possesses

2 Word brings you directly to the top of the next page.

3 If you want to browse by a different type of object, click on the Select Browse Object button.

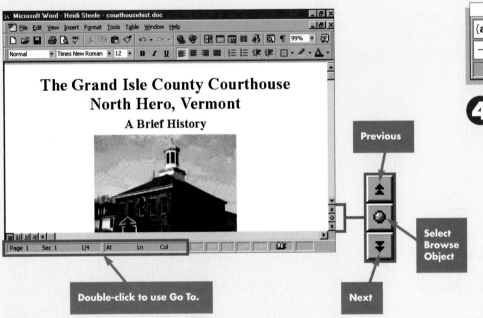

Previous

Select Browse Object

Next

Double-click to use Go To.

Browse by Heading

4 Word displays a grid with squares containing various browse objects. Point to each square to see its description in the gray area at the bottom of the grid. Some objects, such as Field and Comment, are only useful if you have used certain features in your document. The two squares on the left end of the lower row, Go To and Find, display the Find and Replace dialog box. (Go To is described on this page, and Find is described in Chapter 6). Select the object you want—Headings in this example—and click on OK.

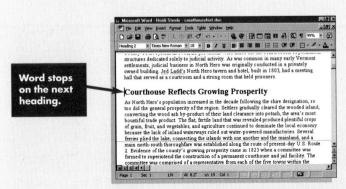

Word stops on the next heading.

6 Clicking on the Next Heading button brings you directly to the next heading in the document. (Word automatically detects what text constitutes a heading.)

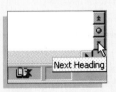

Next Heading

5 As soon as you choose a browse object other than the default choice of Page, the Next and Previous arrows become blue. When you point to the arrows, notice that their ScreenTips reflect the currently selected object.

How to Insert Text

When you insert text, Word normally pushes existing text over to the right to make room for the new text, and adjusts the line breaks within the paragraph to accommodate the insertion. This is almost always how you want Word to behave. Occasionally, however, you may want to use Word's overtype mode. When you're in overtype mode, each character you type *replaces* the character to the right of the insertion point.

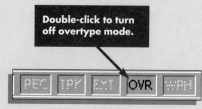

Double-click to turn off overtype mode.

▶ **1** Look at the right-hand portion of the status bar and see whether the overtype notation (OVR) is darkened. If it is, you are currently in overtype mode. To turn the feature off, double-click on OVR or press the Insert key. (You can get into overtype mode at any time by double-clicking OVR or pressing the Insert key again.)

TIP SHEET

▶ It's easy to accidentally get into overtype mode by inadvertently pressing the Insert key, since the Ins key is adjacent to the Home, Del, and End keys on your keyboard. If you notice that existing text is getting deleted as you type, check to see if OVR is darkened (see step 1). If it is, double-click on it to exit overtype mode.

▶ To split a paragraph into two separate paragraphs, place the insertion point where you want the second paragraph to start, and press Enter to insert a paragraph mark. (To add a blank line or two between the paragraphs, press Enter a couple more times.) If you want to join two paragraphs, place the insertion point at the very beginning of the second paragraph, and press Backspace to remove the paragraph mark. (Press Backspace repeatedly if there are blank lines between the paragraphs.) See "How to Type Text in Word" in Chapter 1 to review other ways to use the Enter key.

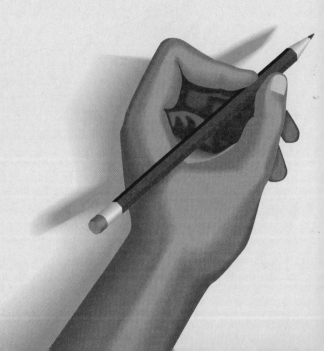

revenues. In fact, the graphs attached
relationship What's more, our adverti
populated otherwise by no-names. As
1998):

2 Position the insertion point where you want to insert text. You can use any of the navigation techniques described earlier in the chapter.

revenues. In fact, the graphs attached suggest a pr
relationship between advertising and revenues W
earn us a reputation in a field populated otherwise
commented (January 12, 1998):

3 Type your insertion. If you started out with the insertion point at the end of an existing word (see step 2), you may need to begin the insertion by adding a space. By the same token, if you began with the insertion point at the beginning of an existing word, you may need to add a space at the end of the inserted text.

LawnBirds, Inc.

ANALYSIS OF OUR ADVERTISING STRATEGY, 1996–1998

INTRODUCTION

It should come as no surprise to any of us that advertising increased our 1996–1998 revenues. In fact, the graphs attached suggest a predictable and even quantifiable relationship. *between advertising and revenues* What's more, our advertising has helped earn us a reputation in a field populated otherwise by no-names. As *Advertising Punditry* commented (January 12, 1998):

> Ask people to name a manufacturer of lawn flamingos and they'll probably draw a blank. But if they don't draw a blank, they'll almost certainly mention LawnBirds, Inc. Thanks to an aggressive multimedia campaign focused squarely on name introduction and reinforcement, LawnBirds has carved an enviable cranny for itself in the consumer's consciousness.

The question, then, is not *whether* advertising sells lawn flamingos. It does. The question is *how many* lawn flamingos advertising sells. Do the increased revenues make up our costs? If they have so far, will they continue to? Do the economics call for increasing our ad budget, stabilizing it, decreasing it, or shifting it among the different media?

This analysis attempts to point our advertising in the right direction for the immediate future. However, we must note one obvious constraint: Any hindsight as to what our revenues and profits would have been without advertising is little more than guesswork. The most we can do is project our growth from our preadvertising years and factor in those marketplace changes that we understand and that are quantifiable.

Why did we start advertising in the first place? It's worthwhile occasionally to remind ourselves why we took the path we took. Recall that in 1991 we saw the arrival of several competitors, many of them with low operating costs and excellent contacts within our

4 Check the punctuation and spacing around the inserted text and edit as necessary. If you need to delete incorrect punctuation or extra spaces, see "How to Delete Text" later in this chapter.

revenues. In fact, the graphs attached suggest a predictable and even quantifiable
relationship between advertising and revenues What's more, our advertising has helped
earn us a reputation in a field populated otherwise by no-names. As *Advertising Punditry*

Adjusted line breaks

5 As you insert text, word wrap adjusts the line breaks for you. The same is true when you delete text.

How to Select Text

To *select* text means to highlight it in preparation for performing some action on it. You already learned in Chapter 2 that you can select text in order to print just that portion of a longer document. Other things you can do to selected text include deleting it, moving it, and formatting it. Steps 1 and 2 explain the most basic way of selecting text: dragging across it with the mouse. While this method always works to select any amount of text, it's frequently not the fastest or easiest way to get the job done. The remaining steps show you some convenient shortcuts for selecting specific amounts of text.

TIP SHEET

▸ To select text using the keyboard, first move the insertion point to one end of the text block. Then, hold down the Shift key and use the arrow keys (or any other key combination described in "How to Navigate in a Document" earlier in this chapter) to move toward the other end of the block, highlighting text as you go. Release the Shift key when the block is selected.

▸ To deselect text without performing an action on it, click anywhere in the text area of the window, or press any arrow key.

▸ After you've selected text and released your mouse, you cannot then drag over the selected block of text to change the size of the selection. If you do, you'll end up *moving* the selected text around your document. Instead, adjust the selection by holding down the Shift key as you press the arrow keys, or click once to deselect and then start over.

The question, then, is not whether advertising sells lawn flamingos. It does. The question is how many lawn flamingos advertising sells. Do the increased revenues make up our costs? If they have so far, will they continue to? Do the economics call for increasing our ad budget, stabilizing it, decreasing it, or shifting it among the different media?

1 Position the mouse pointer at one end of the block of text you want to select.

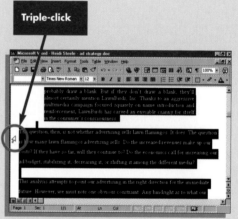

7 To select the entire document, move the mouse pointer to the left of the text, and then triple-click. (You can also choose Edit, Select All, or Ctrl+click while the mouse pointer is to the left of the text.)

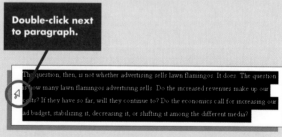

6 To select an individual paragraph, move the mouse pointer to the left of the paragraph (again, the pointer becomes a white arrow pointing to the right), and then double-click.

Drag to select.

> The question, then, is not whether advertising sells lawn flamingos. It does. The question is how many lawn flamingos advertising sells. Do the increased revenues make up our costs? If they have so far, will they continue to? Do the economics call for increasing our ad budget, stabilizing it, decreasing it, or shifting it among the different media?

2 Holding down the left mouse button, drag the mouse toward the other end of the block. If you select too much text, drag the other way to deselect it. When you have the right amount selected, release the mouse button. Now you can issue commands that affect only this text.

Double-click over word.

> The question, then, is not whether advertising sells lawn flamingos. It does. The question is how many lawn flamingos advertising sells. Do the increased revenues make up our costs? If they have so far, will they continue to? Do the economics call for increasing our ad budget, stabilizing it, decreasing it, or shifting it among the different media?

3 To select an individual word, move the mouse pointer anywhere over the word and double-click.

LawnBirds, Inc.

ANALYSIS OF OUR ADVERTISING STRATEGY, 1996–1998

INTRODUCTION

It should come as no surprise to any of us that advertising increased our 1996–1998 revenues. In fact, the graphs attached suggest a predictable and even quantifiable relationship. What's more, our advertising has helped earn us a reputation in a field populated otherwise by no-names. As *Advertising Punditry* commented (January 12, 1998):

> Ask people to name a manufacturer of lawn flamingos and they'll probably draw a blank. But if they don't draw a blank, they'll almost certainly mention LawnBirds, Inc. Thanks to an aggressive multimedia campaign focused squarely on name introduction and reinforcement, LawnBirds has carved an enviable cranny for itself in the consumer's consciousness.

The question, then, is not *whether* advertising sells lawn flamingos. It does. The question is *how many* lawn flamingos advertising sells. Do the increased revenues make up our costs? If they have so far, will they continue to? Do the economics call for increasing our ad budget, stabilizing it, decreasing it, or shifting it among the different media?

This analysis attempts to point our advertising in the right direction for the immediate future. However, we must note one obvious constraint: Any hindsight as to what our revenues and profits would have been without advertising is little more than guesswork. The most we can do is project our growth from our preadvertising years and factor in those marketplace changes that we understand and that are quantifiable.

Why did we start advertising in the first place? It's worthwhile occasionally to remind ourselves why we took the path we took. Recall that in 1991 we saw the arrival of several competitors, many of them with low operating costs and excellent contacts within our

Click next to line.

> The question, then, is not whether advertising sells lawn flamingos. It does. The question is how many lawn flamingos advertising sells. Do the increased revenues make up our costs? If they have so far, will they continue to? Do the economics call for increasing our ad budget, stabilizing it, decreasing it, or shifting it among the different media?

4 To select an individual line, move the mouse pointer to the left of the line—the pointer changes shape to become a white arrow pointing to the right—and then click once.

Ctrl+click over sentence.

> The question, then, is not whether advertising sells lawn flamingos. It does. The question is how many lawn flamingos advertising sells. Do the increased revenues make up our costs? If they have so far, will they continue to? Do the economics call for increasing our ad budget, stabilizing it, decreasing it, or shifting it among the different media?

5 To select a sentence, move the mouse pointer anywhere over the sentence, hold down the Ctrl key and keep it held down as you click the mouse button, then release the Ctrl key.

How to Delete Text

You can delete one character at a time or delete a large block of text by selecting it first. The remaining text shifts over to fill the vacated space, and line breaks adjust automatically. Since Word treats spaces, tabs, and paragraph marks like any other characters, you can also delete them using the techniques shown on this page. And remember, if you delete text accidentally, you can click the Undo button on the Standard toolbar to restore the text (see "How to Undo Actions" in Chapter 3).

The insertion point is just after the text to be deleted.

The insertion point is just before the text to be deleted.

The question, then, is not whether advertising sells lawn flamingos. It does. The question is how many lawn flamingos advertising sells. Do the increased revenues make up our

The question, then, is not whether advertising sells lawn flamingos. It does. The question is how many lawn flamingos advertising sells. Do the increased revenues make up our

1 Position the insertion point just before or after the text you want to delete. Or, select a block of text (see preceding page) if you want to delete the whole block.

TIP SHEET

▸ **To delete the entire word to the right of the insertion point, make sure the insertion point is at the very beginning of the word, and press Ctrl+Del. To delete the entire word to the left of the insertion point, press Ctrl+Backspace. To delete several words, keep the Ctrl key held down while you press Del or Backspace repeatedly.**

▸ **If the character you want to delete is a space, a tab, or a paragraph mark, you may find it helpful to click the Show/Hide button on the Standard toolbar to display these characters on screen (see "How to Type Text in Word" in Chapter 1).**

Pressing Del deleted the letter T.

flamingos. It does. he question

2 If the insertion point is just before the text to be deleted, press the Del key. The Del key deletes the character to the right of the insertion point. You can keep pressing Del to continue deleting to the right, character by character.

Pressing Backspace deleted the period.

flamingos advertising sells Do the

3 If the insertion point is just after the text to be deleted, press the Backspace key. The Backspace key deletes the character to the left of the insertion point. You can keep pressing Backspace to continue deleting to the left, character by character.

LawnBirds, Inc.

ANALYSIS OF OUR ADVERTISING STRATEGY, 1996–1998

INTRODUCTION

It should come as no surprise to any of us that advertising increased our 1996–1998 revenues. In fact, the graphs attached suggest a predictable and even quantifiable relationship. What's more, our advertising has helped earn us a reputation in a field populated otherwise by no-names. As *Advertising Punditry* commented (January 12, 1998):

> Ask people to name a manufacturer of lawn flamingos and they'll probably draw a blank. But if they don't draw a blank, they'll almost certainly mention LawnBirds, Inc. Thanks to an aggressive multimedia campaign focused squarely on name introduction and reinforcement, LawnBirds has carved an enviable cranny for itself in the consumer's consciousness.

The question, then, is not *whether* advertising sells lawn flamingos. It does. ~~The question is *how many* lawn flamingos advertising sells.~~ Do the increased revenues make up our costs? If they have so far, will they continue to? Do the economics call for increasing our ad budget, stabilizing it, decreasing it, or shifting it among the different media?

This analysis attempts to point our advertising in the right direction for the immediate future. However, we must note one obvious constraint: Any hindsight as to what our revenues and profits would have been without advertising is little more than guesswork. The most we can do is project our growth from our preadvertising years and factor in those marketplace changes that we understand and that are quantifiable.

Why did we start advertising in the first place? It's worthwhile occasionally to remind ourselves why we took the path we took. Recall that in 1991 we saw the arrival of several competitors, many of them with low operating costs and excellent contacts within our

Press Backspace or Del to delete the selected text.

The question, then, is not whether advertising sells lawn flamingos. It does. The question is how many lawn flamingos advertising sells. Do the increased revenues make up our

4 To delete a selected block, press the Backspace or Del key.

5 If you want to replace a selected block of text with other text, you don't have to press Backspace or Del before typing the new text. Instead, you can simply start typing; the text you type automatically replaces the selected text.

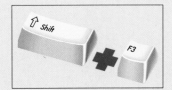

2 Press Shift+F3 one or more times until you see the choice you want, and then click once to deselect the text.

First case conversion

ANALYSIS OF OUR ADVERTISING STRATEGY, 1996–1998

3 Word changes the case the first time.

awnBirds, Inc.

Analysis of Our Advertising Strategy, 1996–1998

awnBirds, Inc.

ANALYSIS OF OUR ADVERTISING STRATEGY, 1996–1998

INTRODUCTION

It should come as no surprise to any of us that advertising increased our 1996–1998 revenues. In fact, the graphs attached suggest a predictable and even quantifiable relationship. What's more, our advertising has helped earn us a reputation in a field populated otherwise by no-names. As *Advertising Punditry* commented (January 12, 1998):

> Ask people to name a manufacturer of lawn flamingos and they'll probably draw a blank. But if they don't draw a blank, they'll almost certainly mention LawnBirds, Inc. Thanks to an aggressive multimedia campaign focused squarely on name introduction and reinforcement, LawnBirds has carved an enviable cranny for itself in the consumer's consciousness.

The question, then, is not *whether* advertising sells lawn flamingos. It does. The question is *how many* lawn flamingos advertising sells. Do the increased revenues make up our costs? If they have so far, will they continue to? Do the economics call for increasing our ad budget, stabilizing it, decreasing it, or shifting it among the different media?

This analysis attempts to point our advertising in the right direction for the immediate future. However, we must note one obvious constraint: Any hindsight as to what our revenues and profits would have been without advertising is little more than guesswork. The most we can do is project our growth from our preadvertising years and factor in those marketplace changes that we understand and that are quantifiable.

Why did we start advertising in the first place? It's worthwhile occasionally to remind ourselves why we took the path we took. Recall that in 1991 we saw the arrival of several competitors, many of them with low operating costs and excellent contacts within our

Second case conversion

analysis of our advertising strategy, 1996-1998

4 Pressing Shift+F3 a second time converts the text again.

Third case conversion

Analysis Of Our Advertising Strategy, 1996-1998

5 Pressing Shift+F3 a third time converts the text one last time. In this example it converts to title case because the selection does not end with a period, exclamation point, or question mark.

ANALYSIS OF OUR ADVERTISING STRATEGY, 1996-1998

6 If you've cycled through all three choices, pressing Shift+F3 again takes you back to the first version.

How to Cut and Copy Using Drag-and-Drop

Dragging text with the mouse is the closest you can get to scooping up text with your hands and dropping it in a new location. You can use it to both cut and copy text (the example on this page shows a cut operation). Drag-and-drop is wonderfully convenient for cutting or copying text short distances—shifting words around in a sentence, or copying a phrase from one sentence to another, for example. It is rather awkward for cutting or copying text over long distances. Read about the cut-and-paste technique described on the next page for an alternative.

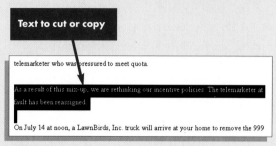

1 Select the text you want to cut or copy (see "How to Select Text" in Chapter 5) and release the mouse button. You can select any amount of text—from one character to the entire document.

7 Deselect the text by clicking once or by pressing an arrow key.

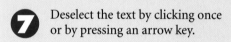

6 When the dotted insertion point is in the proper location, release the mouse button to cut or copy the selected text. (If you're copying the text, make sure you release the mouse button first, and then the Ctrl key.)

TIP SHEET

▶ If you accidentally drop text into the wrong location, you can undo the operation by clicking the Undo button on the Standard toolbar.

▶ Word makes minor adjustments in spacing for you when you cut or copy text. Nonetheless, it's always a good idea to examine text carefully after you've performed a cut or a copy. Make sure the punctuation, spacing, and sentence structure are correct—both at the new location and, if you cut the text, in the vacated spot.

2 Position the mouse pointer over any part of the selected text so that the mouse pointer becomes an arrow.

3 If you want to *cut* the text, press and hold down the left mouse button. A dotted rectangle appears at the bottom of the arrow, and a dotted insertion point appears alongside the arrow.

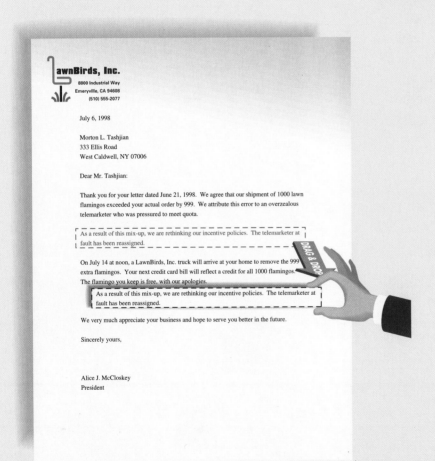

4 If you want to *copy* the text, hold down the Ctrl key while you press and hold down the left mouse button. The mouse pointer shows the same dotted rectangle and insertion point, but it also shows a small plus sign to indicate that you are performing a copy, not a cut.

5 Holding down the mouse button (and the Ctrl key if you're copying), drag the mouse to the place where you want to insert the text. Keep an eye on the dotted insertion point. It tells you where the text will be inserted if you release the mouse at that moment.

How to Cut and Copy Using Cut-and-Paste

While cutting or copying text with the cut-and-paste technique is not quite as fast as using drag-and-drop, it has its advantages. First, all the operations involved, such as selecting text and choosing commands from menus, have direct keyboard equivalents. Second, it is a technique common to almost all Windows-based programs, so you may already be familiar with it. Finally, it is easier than dragging when you are cutting or copying text over a long distance or from one open document to another.

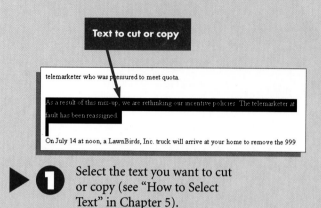

Text to cut or copy

telemarketer who was pressured to meet quota.

As a result of this mix-up, we are rethinking our incentive policies. The telemarketer at fault has been reassigned.

On July 14 at noon, a LawnBirds, Inc. truck will arrive at your home to remove the 999

1 Select the text you want to cut or copy (see "How to Select Text" in Chapter 5).

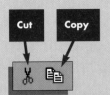

Cut **Copy**

2 If you want to *cut* the text, click on the Cut button in the Standard toolbar (or choose Edit, Cut). The text is deleted from your document, but it remains in a special Windows storage area called the *Clipboard*. If you want to *copy* the text, click on the Copy button in the Standard toolbar (or choose Edit, Copy). When you copy text, nothing appears to happen because the text remains in the original location—but a copy of the selected text is sent to the Clipboard.

Destination

The flamingo you keep

We very much apprecia

Sincerely yours,

3 Place the insertion point where you want to insert the text. If necessary, you can open another document or switch to another already open document to insert text there. (To switch to another open document, click on the Window menu, then click on the document name at the bottom of the menu.)

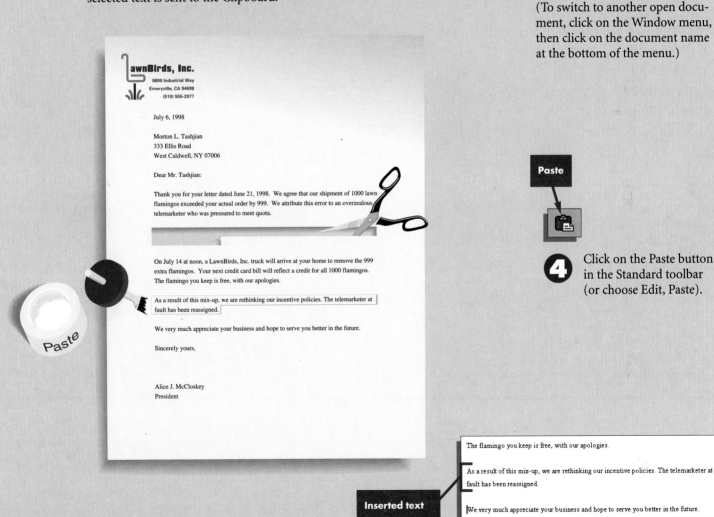

LawnBirds, Inc.
8800 Industrial Way
Emeryville, CA 94608
(510) 555-2077

July 6, 1998

Morton L. Tashjian
333 Ellis Road
West Caldwell, NY 07006

Dear Mr. Tashjian:

Thank you for your letter dated June 21, 1998. We agree that our shipment of 1000 lawn flamingos exceeded your actual order by 999. We attribute this error to an overzealous telemarketer who was pressured to meet quota.

On July 14 at noon, a LawnBirds, Inc. truck will arrive at your home to remove the 999 extra flamingos. Your next credit card bill will reflect a credit for all 1000 flamingos. The flamingo you keep is free, with our apologies.

As a result of this mix-up, we are rethinking our incentive policies. The telemarketer at fault has been reassigned.

We very much appreciate your business and hope to serve you better in the future.

Sincerely yours,

Alice J. McCloskey
President

Paste

4 Click on the Paste button in the Standard toolbar (or choose Edit, Paste).

Inserted text

The flamingo you keep is free, with our apologies.

As a result of this mix-up, we are rethinking our incentive policies. The telemarketer at fault has been reassigned.

We very much appreciate your business and hope to serve you better in the future.

5 The text is pasted into the document at the position of the insertion point. In a Cut operation such as the one shown on this page, the text is removed from the original location. If you perform a Copy operation, the text remains in its original location.

How to Find Text Automatically

Anyone who frequently creates long documents has probably had the experience of scrolling through a document trying to find all the places where you used a particular word or phrase. Scanning a long document line-by-line can be a painstakingly slow process, and no matter how careful you are, it's likely that you'll miss something. Thankfully, Word's find feature can do this kind of job for you, and it is faster and more accurate than we humans could ever hope to be.

1 Choose Edit, Find to display the Find and Replace dialog box with the Find tab in front (or double-click anywhere on the left two-thirds of status bar, and then click on the Find tab).

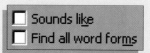

8 Sounds Like finds words that sound like the text you're searching for; use this option if you're not sure of the spelling. Find All Word Forms finds all forms of the word. For example, if you search for *sing*, Word will also find *sings*, *sang*, *sung*, and *singing*.

Use wildcards

7 Mark the Use Wildcards check box if you want to use wildcard characters in the Find What text. You can enter wildcards by typing them directly, or by clicking on the Special button and choosing them from a list. If you aren't sure what a wildcard is or how to use one, ask the Office Assistant to look up information on Find and Replace in Word's help system. (See Chapter 3 for help on using the Office Assistant.)

TIP SHEET

▶ The Find and Replace dialog box lets you to edit your document while the dialog box is on screen. Click outside the dialog box to activate the document, and make the desired changes. When you're finished, click the title bar of the Find and Replace dialog box to activate it again.

▶ You can use the Format button in the Find and Replace dialog box to look for specific formatting in your document. (You'll learn how to format your documents in upcoming chapters.)

▶ The Special button in the Find and Replace dialog box lets you look for special characters such as paragraph marks and tabs.

Type the text you want to find in the Find What text box, and click on the Find Next button.

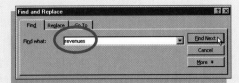

 awnBirds, Inc.

Analysis of Our Advertising Strategy, 1996–1998

INTRODUCTION

It should come as no surprise to any of us that advertising increased our 1996–1998 revenues. In fact, the graphs attached suggest a predictable and even quantifiable relationship. What's more, our advertising has helped earn us a reputation in a field populated otherwise by no-names. As *Advertising Punditry* commented (January 12, 1998):

> Ask people to name a manufacturer of lawn flamingos and they'll probably draw a blank. But if they don't draw a blank, they'll almost certainly mention LawnBirds, Inc. Thanks to an aggressive multimedia campaign focused squarely on name introduction and reinforcement, LawnBirds has carved an enviable cranny for itself in the consumer's consciousness.

The question, then, is not *whether* advertising sells lawn flamingos. It does. The question is *how many* lawn flamingos advertising sells. Do the increased revenues make up our costs? If they have so far, will they continue to? Do the economics call for increasing our ad budget, stabilizing it, decreasing it, or shifting it among the different media?

This analysis attempts to point our advertising in the right direction for the immediate future. However, we must note one obvious constraint: Any hindsight as to what our revenues and profits would have been without advertising is little more than guesswork. The most we can do is project our growth from our preadvertising years and factor in those marketplace changes that we understand and that are quantifiable.

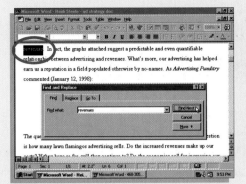

3 Word highlights the first occurrence of the word. Continue clicking Find Next to look for more matches. When Word has found all the matching words, it informs you that it has finished searching the document. Click on OK to return to the Find and Replace dialog box, and then click on the Cancel button to return to your document.

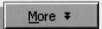

4 If you want to be more specific about what text you're looking for, click on the More button to expand the Find and Replace dialog box. (You can shrink the dialog box to its original size at any time by clicking on the Less button.)

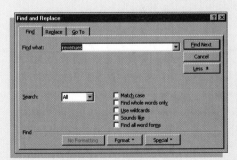

5 Word displays several options for customizing the search. By default, Word searches the entire document for the Find What text. If you only want to search up or down from the location of the insertion point, change the option in the Search drop-down list.

 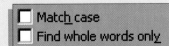 Use Match Case to find only occurrences of the text that have the same combination of upper and lowercase letters you typed in the Find What box. Use Find Whole Words Only if you don't want Word to find the search text when it's part of another word. For example, you'd mark this check box if you wanted to find only the word *cat*, not *catch*, *decathlon*, or *scathing*.

How to Replace Text Automatically

Sometimes you not only need to find text, you also have to replace it with something else. Let's say you wrote a 20-page proposal for a client, and then discovered that you'd misspelled the name of the client's company. Rather than manually finding and fixing the name in dozens of places, you could use the Replace feature instead. Whenever you find yourself about to change something by hand in a several places in a document, stop and see if you could have Replace make the change for you.

▶ **1** Choose Edit, Replace to display the Find and Replace dialog box with the Replace tab in front (or double-click anywhere on the left two-thirds of status bar, and then click on the Replace tab).

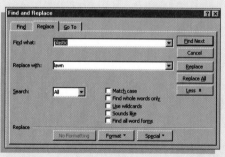

7 Change the selection in the Search list if desired, and mark one or more of the check boxes in the middle of the dialog box. For descriptions of what each option does, refer to steps 5 through 8 on the previous page.

6 Optionally, click the More button to expand the dialog box and display options for customizing how the replace feature works. (You can click on the Less button at any time to shrink the dialog box to its original size.)

2 Type the text you want to find in the Find What text box.

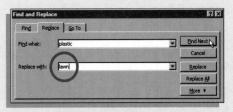

3 In the Replace With text box, type the text that will replace the Find What text. Click on the Find Next button.

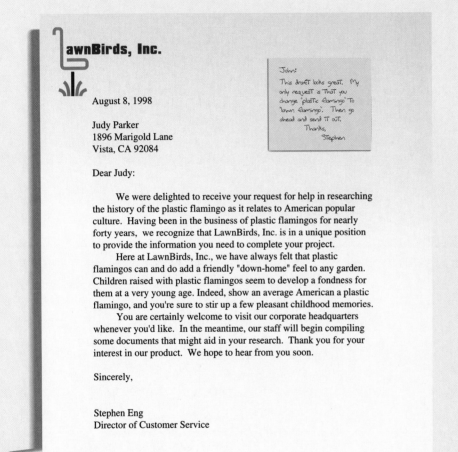

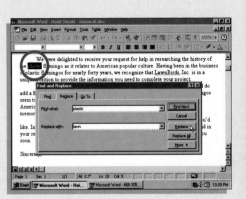

4 Word highlights the first matching word. To replace the word, click the Replace button. (If you don't want to replace this word, click Find Next again to find the next matching word.) Repeat this process as many times as necessary. When Word displays a message box stating that "Word has finished searching the document," click on OK to return to the Find and Replace dialog box, and then click on the Close button to return to your document.

5 If you want to make the change throughout the whole document without confirming each replacement, click on the Replace All button instead of Find Next in the step 3. If you use Replace All, Word tells you how many replacements it made when it finishes the find and replace process.

CHAPTER 7

Corrurecting Your Spelling and Grammar

Word gives you three different ways to check and correct the spelling and grammar in your document, all of them well designed and simple to use. After you've experimented with the various techniques, you'll probably end up using some combination of all three.

You may have seen the first feature, automatic spell and grammar checking, doing its job already. As you're typing, it marks possible misspellings and grammatical problems so that you can easily find and correct them. Word gives you a list of suggestions for the spellings or grammatical fixes—all you have to do is click on the option you want, and Word makes the change for you.

Alternatively, you can wait until you've typed the whole document, and then use the standard spelling and grammar checker to check the entire document all at once. If you've used Word or other word processing programs before, you're probably familiar with this method of spell and grammar checking.

Finally, you can use AutoCorrect to fix commonly misspelled words automatically. If there's a word you have a habit of spelling incorrectly, you can give AutoCorrect both the misspelled and the correctly spelled versions of the word, and from then on Word will fix the spelling for you without your having to issue any command at all.

How to Correct Spelling and Grammar "On the Fly"

Automatic spell and grammar checking monitors the characters you type. As soon as you type a word that is not in Word's dictionary or doesn't conform to one of Word's grammatical rules and then continue typing or move somewhere else in the document, Word places a colored wavy line under the word to mark it as a possible mistake. It uses red to mark spelling errors and green to mark grammar problems.

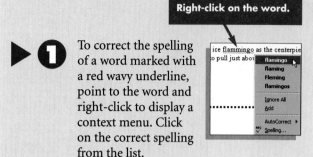

1 To correct the spelling of a word marked with a red wavy underline, point to the word and right-click to display a context menu. Click on the correct spelling from the list.

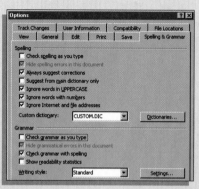

8 If you don't want to use automatic spell and grammar checking in any document, clear the check boxes labeled Check Spelling As You Type and Check Grammar As You Type. Then click on OK.

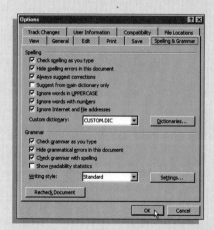

7 Mark the Hide Spelling Errors in This Document check box if you want to temporarily hide the red wavy lines in the current document, and mark the Hide Grammar Errors in This Document check box to hide the green wavy lines. Then click on OK.

TIP SHEET

▶ If a word marked with a red wavy underline is spelled correctly and you use the word frequently, click on Add in the context menu to add it to the dictionary. This way, Word won't mark it in future documents.

▶ If a word with a red wavy underline is spelled correctly but you don't use it that often, you may want to choose Ignore All from the context menu. This prevents Word from marking that word wherever it appears in the current document, but doesn't add the word to the dictionary.

▶ If a word is marked with a green wavy line and you choose Ignore Sentence from the context menu, Word simply removes the wavy line, but it continues to mark other similar grammatical errors it finds in the document.

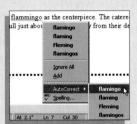

2 If the mistake is one you make frequently, you can choose AutoCorrect from the context menu and then click on the correct spelling in the submenu to add this correction to the AutoCorrect dialog box. Then in the future, when you type the misspelling, Word corrects it automatically. You'll learn more about AutoCorrect in the last topic of this chapter.

Right-click on the phrase or word.

3 To fix the grammar of a word or phrase marked with a green wavy line, right-click to display a context menu, and click on the desired correction.

> Meanwhile, I'll reserve the auditorium and look into catering. I was thinking we could order a carved ice flamingo as the centerpiece. The catered food, along with some live music, is sure to pull just about everyone away from their desks.

4 Word corrects the spelling and grammatical mistakes for you.

5 You can move from one spelling/grammar error to the next in the document by double-clicking on the Spelling and Grammar Error Status icon—the little book in the lower-right corner of the Word window. Each time you double-click on the icon, Word moves to the next mistake and displays the context menu you normally display by right-clicking on the word or phrase.

6 To hide or disable automatic spell and grammar checking, choose Tools, Options, and click on the Spelling & Grammar tab.

How to Use the Spelling and Grammar Checker

The spelling and grammar checker lets you check the spelling and grammar of an entire document all at once. If your document is several pages long, this method might be quicker than correcting words one by one (see the preceding page). If you want additional grammar coaching as you're checking your document, display the Office Assistant (see Chapter 3). It will give you examples and advice relating to any grammatical problems Word finds.

TIP SHEET

▶ **To check the spelling and grammar of only a portion of the document, select that portion before starting the check. When Word finishes checking the selection, it asks if you want to check the rest of the document. Click the No button to end the check.**

▶ **To modify what Word looks for in a grammar check, choose Tools, Options, and click on the Spelling & Grammar tab. In the Writing Style drop-down list, select the style—casual, technical, formal, and so on—that best describes your document. Optionally, you can hand pick which items Word checks by clicking on the Settings button. In the Grammar Settings dialog box, mark or clear check boxes for items such as Wordiness, Relative Clauses, and Passive Sentences, make punctuation-related choices in the drop-down lists, and click on OK.**

▶ **1** Click on the Spelling and Grammar button on the Standard toolbar (or choose Tools, Spelling and Grammar). Word begins checking every word in your document against its dictionary and list of grammatical rules.

8 Choose the Ignore button if you don't want to change the word or phrase; choose Ignore All to have Word ignore the same text if it appears elsewhere in your document. Word informs you when the spelling and grammar check is complete (either via the Office Assistant or a message box). Click on OK to close the message box (or click outside the Office Assistant).

7 When Word encounters a possible grammatical error, it displays the word and the surrounding text at the top of the dialog box and gives you a description of the problem—*Commonly Confused Words* in this example. If you see the correct version in the Suggestions list, click on it and click on the Change button. (If you don't see the correct version, edit the phrase in the upper part of the dialog box, and then click on the Change button.)

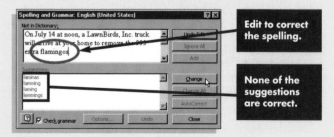

Edit to correct the spelling.

None of the suggestions are correct.

6 If the word is misspelled but the correct spelling is not in the Suggestions list, double-click on the misspelled word at the top of the dialog box to select it, and type over it with the correct spelling. Then click on the Change button.

2 Word presents the Spelling and Grammar dialog box when it encounters a word that is not in its dictionary or does not conform to a grammatical rule.

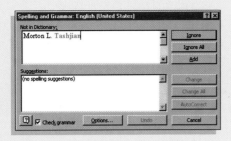

3 If the problem is spelling-related, Word displays the word and its surrounding text in a text box labeled Not in Dictionary. If the word is spelled correctly but you don't expect to use it often, click on the Ignore button to skip over the word. To prevent Word from stopping on other instances of the same word in the document, click on Ignore All. Because these two buttons do not add the word to the dictionary, the spelling and grammar checker will question the word in other documents.

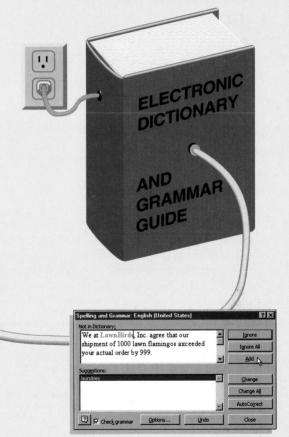

5 If the word is misspelled and you see the correct spelling in the Suggestions list, click on the spelling you want, and click on the Change button to correct the word. (Click on the Change All button to have Word correct all instances of this misspelled word in your document.)

4 If the word is correctly spelled and you plan to use it frequently in other documents, click on the Add button. This adds the word to the dictionary so that Word won't question it when you run spelling and grammar checks on other documents.

How to Fix Spelling with AutoCorrect

There are probably a few typos that you seem to repeat over and over. Or maybe there are some words you can't for the life of you remember how to spell. AutoCorrect not only takes the tedium out of fixing these kinds of mistakes, it can even be used as a shortcut for typing symbols, long names, or phrases. AutoCorrect already knows how to correct many misspelled words; this page shows you how to add your own entries to the list.

▶ **1** Choose Tools, AutoCorrect to display the AutoCorrect dialog box.

▶ **The upper portion of the AutoCorrect dialog box contains several options for fixing common typing mistakes. You can pick and choose which of these options you want to use, but make sure to keep the Replace Text As You Type check box marked. Otherwise, AutoCorrect won't automatically fix your mistakes.**

▶ **To delete an AutoCorrect entry, display the AutoCorrect dialog box, select the entry you want to delete in the list, click on the Delete button, and then click on OK.**

▶ **You cannot include a space at the end of an entry in the Replace text box. (If you do accidentally, Word dims the Add button to prevent you from adding the entry.) However, you can include spaces *between* words. For example, you could type *int he* in the Replace text box and *in the* in the With text box.**

Please contact the napf

Please contact the National Association of Poodle Fanciers

8 Now when you type the abbreviation and press the spacebar, Word automatically converts it to the full spelling.

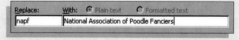

Replace: napf   With: National Association of Poodle Fanciers

7 You can create AutoCorrect entries that function as shortcuts for typing long names. To do this, type an abbreviation for the name in the Replace text box. (Use some abbreviation that you don't want to leave as is in your documents, since every time you type it, AutoCorrect will automatically convert it to the entry in the With text box.) Type the full version of the name in the With text box, click on Add, and then click on OK.

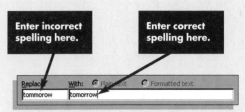

2 Scroll through the list at the bottom of the dialog box to see what things AutoCorrect already knows how to fix. When you type any of the entries in the left column, Word automatically replaces them with the corresponding entries to the right. Notice that the top of the list contains shortcuts for inserting various symbols. (For example, if you type *(tm)*, Word places it with the trademark symbol ™. Further down in the list are many commonly misspelled words.

Enter incorrect spelling here.

Enter correct spelling here.

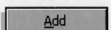

3 To add an entry, click in the Replace text box and type the word as you normally misspell it. Then click in the With text box and type the correct spelling.

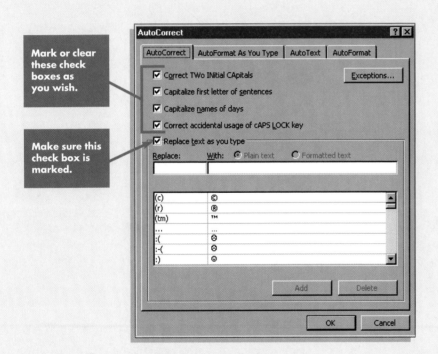

Mark or clear these check boxes as you wish.

Make sure this check box is marked.

Add

4 Click on the Add button to add the new entry to the list.

OK

5 Click on the OK button to close the dialog box and return to your document.

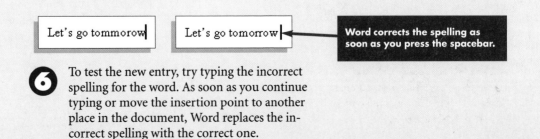

Word corrects the spelling as soon as you press the spacebar.

6 To test the new entry, try typing the incorrect spelling for the word. As soon as you continue typing or move the insertion point to another place in the document, Word replaces the incorrect spelling with the correct one.

TRY IT!

You've built up a solid base of editing skills using the previous four chapters of this book. Here is an opportunity to get some hands-on practice. Follow these steps at your computer to type, edit, and print the document shown. Keep in mind that the line breaks in your paragraphs will not match those shown here—the lines of text in the figures were shortened to make the text easier to read. Also remember that Word's formatting options can be modified easily, so depending on what settings you or someone else has chosen on your computer, your sample document may not match the one shown here in every detail.

1

With Word running, start a new document.

LawnBirds, Inc.
8800 Industrial Way
Emeryville, CA 94608
(510) 555-2077

July 6, 1996

Mae Thorpe
1073 San Gabriel Avenue
San Francisco, CA 94112

Dear Ms. Thorpe:

We are sorry to hear about the unfortunate discoloration of your LawnBirds, Inc., lawn flamingo. You may find it of minor consolation to know that spontaneous mutations have indeed produced beige flamingos in the wild.

Please return the flamingo to the address above at your earliest convenience and we will be happy to send you a pink one fresh from the assembly line. We have developed a new chemical process that should prevent discoloration in the future.

Again, we at LawnBirds, Inc., apologize for the inconvenience. We hope to have the opportunity to serve you better in the future.

Sincerely yours,

Stephen Eng
Director of Customer Service

2

July 6, 1998

Mae Thorpe
1073 San Gabriel Avenue
San Francisco, CA 94112

Dear Ms. Thorpe|

Type the date,
press Enter
twice, type the recipient's name and
address as shown, press Enter twice,
and then type **Dear Ms. Thorpe:**.

3

We are crestfallen to hear about the unfortunate
discoloration of your LawnBirds, Inc. flamingo. You may
find it of minor consolation to know that spontaneous
mutations have indeed produced beige-tinted flamingos in
the wild.|

Press Enter
twice, press Tab, and type
the paragraph shown here.

4

July 6, 1998

Mae Thorpe
1073 San Gabriel Avenue
San Francisco, CA 94112

Dear Ms. Thorpe:

    We are crestfallen to hear about the unfortunate
discoloration of your LawnBirds, Inc. flamingo. You may
find it of minor consolation to know that spontaneous
mutations have indeed produced beige-tinted flamingos in
the wild.

Double-click
on the word
crestfallen to
select it and
type **sorry** to
replace this
word.

5

    We are sorry to hear about the unfortunate
discoloration of your LawnBirds, Inc. flamingo. You may
find it of minor consolation to know that spontaneous
mutations have indeed produced beige-tinted flamingos in
the wild.

Drag over *-tinted*
in the hyphenated compound *beige-
tinted* to select it and press the Delete
key to delete the selected text. Add a
space after *beige* if necessary.

6

    We have developed a new chemical process that
should prevent discoloration in the future. Please return the
flamingo to the address above at your earliest convenience
and we will be happy to send you a pink one fresh from the
assembly line.|

Press Ctrl+End
to move the insertion point to the end of
the document. Then press Enter, press Tab,
and type the paragraph shown here.

7

    We have developed a new chemical process that
should prevent discoloration in the future. Please return the
flamingo to the address above at your earliest convenience
and we will be happy to send you a pink one fresh from the
assembly line.

Select the second sentence in
the paragraph you just typed.

8

We have developed
should prevent discoloration
flamingo to the address abo

Point to the selected sentence, hold
down the left mouse button, and
drag until the dotted vertical bar is
at the beginning of the paragraph.

Continue to next page ▶

TRY IT!

**Continue
below**

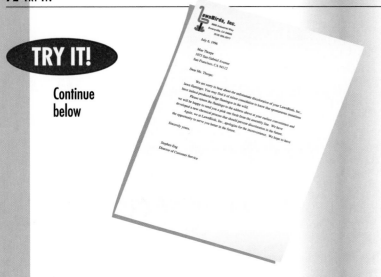

9

Release the
mouse button to
move the sentence.

10

Click to remove the selection, and
then add a space between the two
sentences in the paragraph.

11

Press Ctrl+End to move the insertion
point to the end of the document.
Then press Enter, press Tab, and type
the beginning of the last paragraph
Again, we at followed by a space.

12

In the first
paragraph, select *LawnBirds,
Inc.* including the period.

13

Click on the Copy button in
the Standard toolbar to send
a copy of the selected words
to the Clipboard.

14

Press Ctrl+End, and then
click on the Paste button
in the Standard toolbar
to insert *LawnBirds, Inc.*
in the document.

15

Finish typing
the docu-
ment, being
sure to misspell
apologize as
shown.

16

Click the Spelling and Grammar button in the Standard toolbar.

17

When Word alerts you to correctly spelled words such as *Gabriel* and *LawnBirds*, or to phrases whose grammar you don't want to change, click on the Ignore button.

18

When Word points out misspelled words such as *apollogize*, click on the correct spelling in the Suggestions list (or if none of the suggestions are correct, edit the word in the Not in Dictionary box), and then click on the Change button.

19

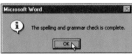

When Word tells you that the spelling and grammar check is complete, click on the OK button.

20

Click on the Print Preview button on the Standard toolbar.

21

If necessary, click on the One Page button in the Print Preview toolbar (the third button from the left) to adjust the magnification of the page to the size shown here. If you like, click on the page twice to zoom in and out. Then click on the Close button in the Print Preview toolbar.

22

Print one copy of the document.

23

Save the document under the name *Beige Flamingos*.

24

Close the document.

CHAPTER 8

Entering Text Automatically

Almost all word processing programs offer ways to enter text automatically. However, the features are often so complicated that many people opt not to use them, in favor of typing everything "by hand." Fortunately, Word's automatic-text features are quite easy to learn; you only need to invest a few minutes of time getting up to speed on skills that will save you hours down the road.

This chapter begins with a description of Word's automatic date feature. You learn how to insert the date as regular text and as a *field*, which gets updated to the current day's date whenever you open the document. And with the help of AutoComplete, you can have Word insert the date without even issuing a command.

The second and third topics of this chapter explain Word's AutoText feature. *AutoText* "memorizes" blocks of text you type frequently as separate AutoText entries. You might want to create AutoText entries for such things as a paragraph of legalese, a description of your products and services, or the closing of a letter. To insert an entry in your document, you simply begin typing its name, and AutoComplete replaces the name with the actual block of text. AutoText entries can include any combination of text and graphics.

AutoText entries not only save time, they cut down on proofreading as well. You only have to proof a block of text carefully when you're creating the entry. From then on, you insert the same entry over and over, so you can rest assured that it's still error-free.

How to Insert the Date Automatically

Your computer has a clock that keeps track of both the date and the time. Instead of typing the current date, you can have Word take this information from your computer and insert it in your document. You can even insert the date as a *field* (a holding place for information—in this case, the date) and let Word update the date automatically when you open the document. That way, if you typed the document yesterday, but print it today, it will contain today's date.

1 One way to insert the current day's date is to take advantage of Word's AutoComplete feature. Move the insertion point to the desired location, type the month, and press the spacebar. An AutoComplete tip appears suggesting the current date. Press Enter to let Word complete the date for you.

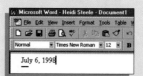

7 Word inserts the date in your document.

6 Click on the OK button in the Date and Time dialog box.

5 Click on the Yes button when Word confirms that you want to change the default date format.

2 If you want to choose a different date format or insert the date as a field, choose Insert, Date and Time.

3 Word presents the Date and Time dialog box, which lists a variety of formats in which you can display the date and/or time. To insert a date as a field so that it will be updated each time you open the document, mark the Update Automatically check box. Make sure this check box is cleared if you want to insert the date as normal text that will not be updated when you open the document in the future.

4 Click on the date format you want to use. If you think you'll use this format most of the time, you might want to make it the default. Word uses the default format whenever you insert the date with the keyboard shortcut Alt+Shift+D. If you don't specify a default date format, Word uses the first format listed in the Date and Time dialog box. To make the selected format your default, click on the Default button.

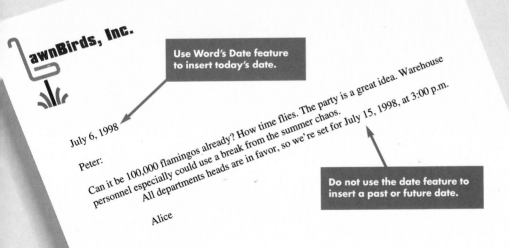

LawnBirds, Inc.

Use Word's Date feature to insert today's date.

July 6, 1998

Peter:

Can it be 100,000 flamingos already? How time flies. The party is a great idea. Warehouse personnel especially could use a break from the summer chaos. All departments heads are in favor, so we're set for July 15, 1998, at 3:00 p.m.

Do not use the date feature to insert a past or future date.

Alice

How to Create and Use Your Own AutoText Entries

AutoText entries can be of any length, from a short sentence to an entire letter. Word organizes AutoText entries according to the style of the first paragraph in the entry. (A *style* is a collection of formatting codes that has been assigned a name. You'll learn how to create and use styles in Chapter 13.) The default style in Word documents is *Normal,* so unless you use other styles, all your AutoText entries will be stored with the Normal style.

TIP SHEET

▶ **This page and the next show you how to use the AutoText toolbar. However, you can also issue AutoText-related commands via the Insert, AutoText menu.**

▶ **You can print a list of AutoText entries to help you remember what text each entry contains. Choose File, Print, and display the Print What list in the lower-left corner of the Print dialog box. Click on AutoText Entries, and then click on OK.**

▶ **In step 7, if you see a button name other than All Entries, read steps 3 and 4 on the next page for an explanation.**

▶ **Unless you tell Word otherwise, Word makes your AutoText entries accessible to all documents. It does this by saving your entries in the *Normal template,* also known as the *Blank Document template.* (See Chapter 14 for more on templates.)**

▶ **To modify the text of an AutoText entry, first insert it in your document, then make your changes. Select the text again, being sure to include all the text you want in the entry, not just the part you modified. Click on the New button in the AutoText toolbar, type the name of the existing entry, and click on OK. When Word asks if you want to redefine the AutoText entry, click on Yes.**

▶ ① If the AutoText toolbar isn't already displayed, choose View, Toolbars, AutoText to bring it into view.

❽ To delete an AutoText entry, click on the AutoText button at the left edge of the AutoText toolbar to display the AutoText tab of the AutoCorrect dialog box. Click on the entry, click on the Delete button, and click on OK.

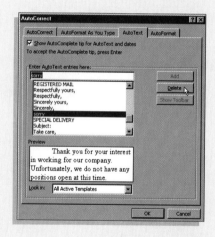

❼ You can also insert AutoText entries from the AutoText toolbar. Click on the All Entries button to display a list of categories of AutoText entries. Many of these categories contain entries that come with Word (see the next page). The ones you have created will be listed under Normal (and possibly other style names, depending on what entries you have created). Point to the style name, and then click on the desired entry in the submenu.

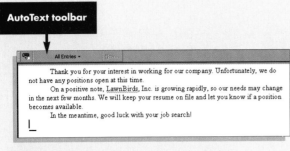

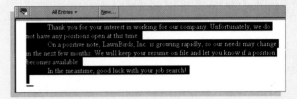

2 Type the text you want to include in your AutoText entry.

3 Select the text. If you want to include any paragraph formatting you've applied, such as line spacing, indents, or alignment (see Chapter 10), be sure to include the paragraph mark at the end of the text. (You might find it useful to click on the Show/Hide button in the Standard toolbar to display paragraph marks.)

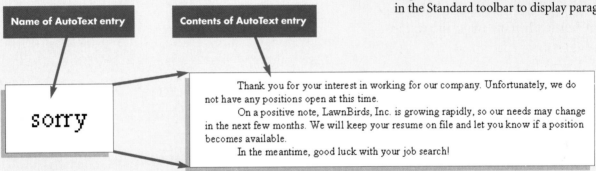

4 Click on the New button in the AutoText toolbar (or choose Insert, AutoText, New).

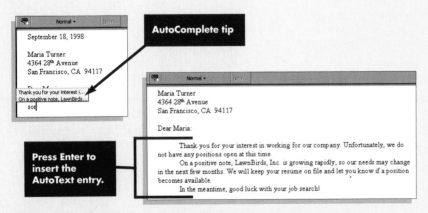

5 In the Create AutoText dialog box, type a name for the entry in the text box labeled Please Name Your AutoText Entry, and click on OK. It's best to choose a name that's short and easy to type (although Word allows AutoText names that are more than one word long).

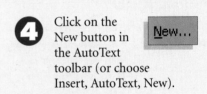

6 To use the entry, click at the desired location in your document and begin typing the name. After you type the first three characters, an AutoComplete tip appears with a snippet of the entry. Press Enter to insert the entry in your document. (You can also type the entry's name and press F3.)

How to Use Word's AutoText Entries

In addition to creating and using your own AutoText entries (see preceding page) you can also use the default entries that come with Word. Word's entries are a little different than user-defined ones in that the entries don't have names. To use one of them, you can either select it from a list, or, if you know the first few characters of the entry, you can just begin typing it and let AutoComplete fill in the rest.

▶ ❶ If the AutoText toolbar isn't already displayed, choose View, Toolbars, AutoText.

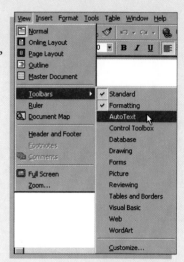

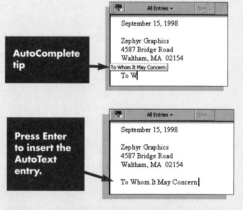

AutoComplete tip

Press Enter to insert the AutoText entry.

❼ If you already know how one of Word's default AutoText entries begins, you can simply type the first few characters of the entry. As soon an AutoComplete tip appears, press Enter to insert the remainder of the entry.

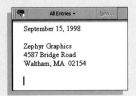

2 Move the insertion point to the place in the document where you want to insert the AutoText entry.

3 Observe the long button in the AutoText toolbar. If the button name is something other than All Entries, skip to the next step. If the name is All Entries, it means your insertion point is resting in a paragraph formatted with the default Normal style. When you click on the All Entries button, Word displays a list containing all AutoText entries, both the ones that come with Word and the ones you've created.

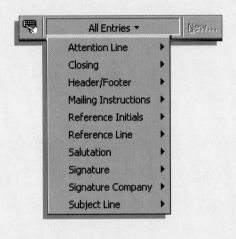

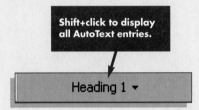

4 If the button has a name other than All Entries (Heading 1 in this example), it means your insertion point is resting in a paragraph that's formatted with some style other than Normal. If you click on the button, Word only displays AutoText entries for that particular style. To display the full list of AutoText entries, Shift+click on the button.

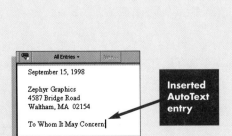

Inserted AutoText entry

6 The entry is inserted in your document.

5 The AutoText entries that come with Word are arranged in categories such as Attention Line, Closing, and Header/Footer. If you have created your own entries, they are organized by style name. In the example shown here, Body Text, Heading 1, and Normal are names of styles that contain user-defined AutoText entries. Point to a category to display its submenu of AutoText entries, then click on the desired entry.

CHAPTER 9

Character Formatting

 This chapter is the first of three on formatting. *Formatting* refers to all the techniques that enhance the appearance of your document. In Word, you can roughly divide formatting techniques into three categories: character, paragraph, and page.

Character formatting includes all the features that can affect individual characters; the primary character formatting features are boldface, italic, underline, font, and font size. In Chapter 10, you'll learn about paragraph formatting. Features that fall into this category include line spacing, indents, alignment, tabs, and so on. The third category, page formatting, is covered in Chapter 11. Some examples of page formatting features are margins, page breaks, and paper size.

In this chapter and the next, you'll frequently learn two methods of accomplishing the same task—one using the Formatting toolbar and the other using a dialog box. Toolbar buttons are convenient because they let you apply formatting quickly. On the other hand, you'll probably prefer to use dialog boxes at times because they let you change several settings at once, and they allow you to preview the changes before applying them to your text. If you're in a hurry, by all means use the Formatting toolbar to get the job done. But if you have the time, go ahead and try out both methods. It never hurts to expand your repertoire.

How to Boldface, Italicize, and Underline Text

Word refers to boldface, italic, and underline as *font styles*. You can use font styles separately or in combination. For example, you could both boldface and italicize a heading. As you experiment with font styles, keep in mind that you should use them sparingly. A little boldface, italic, or underline in a few places can add just the right emphasis to a document, but too much makes a document difficult to read. The first three steps on this page show you how to add font styles quickly using the Formatting toolbar. The remaining steps show you how to make the same changes in the Font dialog box.

1 To boldface text, select the text and then click on the Bold button on the Formatting toolbar.

8 When you've made your selections, click on the OK button to close the dialog box and apply the changes to the selected text.

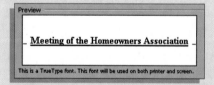

7 You can preview your choices in the Preview area at the bottom of the dialog box.

▶ **To remove boldface, italics, or underline, select the text, and then click on the appropriate button again.**

▶ **If you don't feel like reaching for your mouse, you can apply font styles by selecting the text, then using one of the following keyboard shortcuts: Ctrl+B for boldface, Ctrl+I for italics, Ctrl+U for underline, or Ctrl+Shift+D for double underline. You can also type asterisks before and after a word to boldface it (as in *poodle*) or type underscore characters before and after a word to underline it (as in _poodle_). As soon as you type the next word, Word deletes the asterisks or underscores and applies the formatting.**

▶ **If you want to boldface, italicize, or underline a single word, you don't have to select the word first. Just click anywhere in the word, and then apply the formatting using any of the methods described on this page.**

2 To italicize text, select the text and then click on the Italic button on the Formatting toolbar.

3 To underline text, select the text and then click on the Underline button on the Formatting toolbar. The Underline button produces a single underline. If you want a different type of underlining, use the Font dialog box instead, as described in the remaining steps on this page.

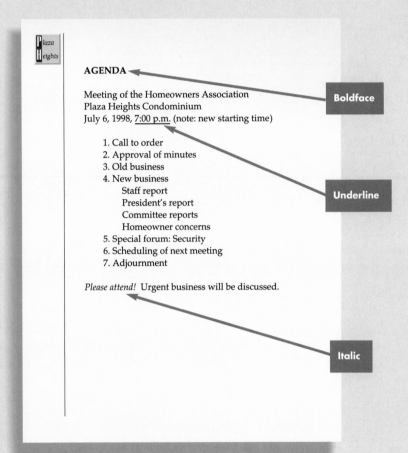

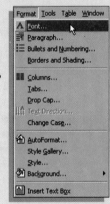

4 If you want to see what a font style will look like before applying it, first select the text, and then choose Format, Font to display the Font dialog box.

6 To underline text, click on the down arrow to the right of the Underline list box to display the list of choices, and click on the desired underline style.

5 At the top of the dialog box, click on the Font tab if it isn't already in front. Then in the Font Style list, choose Bold, Italic, or Bold Italic to boldface and/or italicize your text.

How to Change Fonts

For many people, fiddling with fonts is one of the more entertaining aspects of word processing. However, it's easy to go overboard and format the document within an inch of its life. Resist this temptation! Two fonts per document is usually enough. The first three steps on this page describe how to change fonts using the Formatting toolbar. The remaining steps show you how to use the Font dialog box, which lets you see what fonts will look like before you apply them to your text.

TIP SHEET

▸ **The number and type of available fonts can vary from one computer to the next, but most computers have a wide selection of TrueType fonts. They're displayed in font lists with a TT symbol next to their names. TrueType fonts are good ones to use because they look the same on screen as they do when printed out.**

▸ **If you want to spice up the appearance of a heading, try some of the special effects in the Effects area of the Font dialog box. Shadow, Outline, Emboss, and Engrave can all add a nice decorative touch to small blocks of text.**

▸ **The settings in the Formatting toolbar—for font, font size, font style, and so on—show you the formatting *at the location of the insertion point*. This behavior comes in handy when you aren't sure what font is applied to a particular block of text. All you have to do is click in the text to place the insertion point there, and then look at the Formatting toolbar to see what settings are in effect.**

▸ **The keyboard shortcut to display the Font dialog box is Ctrl+D.**

▶ **1** Select the text whose font you want to change.

7 When you've found the right one, click on it, and then click on OK to close the dialog box and apply the font to the selected text.

Times New Roman ▼

② Click on the down arrow to the right of the Font list box in the Formatting toolbar to display a list of your fonts.

③ Scroll through the list to find the font you want, and then click on it to apply it to the selected text. Note that Word places the fonts you use frequently above a double line at the top of the list. Below the double line is an alphabetical list of all the fonts.

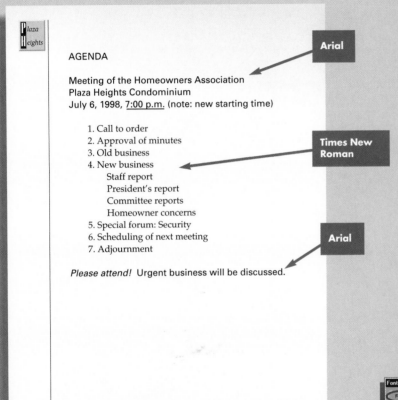

Arial

Times New Roman

Arial

④ If you want to preview the various fonts before choosing one, first select the text, and then choose Format, Font to display the Font dialog box.

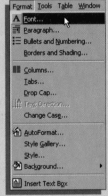

⑥ Try clicking on a few fonts; you can see what each one looks like in the Preview area at the bottom of the dialog box.

⑤ Click on the Font tab at the top of the dialog box if it isn't already in front. Scroll through the Font list to see your choices.

How to Change Font Size

Most type in books and periodicals is 10, 11, or 12 points high. Word assumes a 10-point font for new documents. In the sample document shown on this page, the body text has been changed to 12-point (notice that a *12* is displayed in the Font list box in step 2). As with the previous pages in this chapter, the first three steps explain how to change font size using the Formatting toolbar, and the remaining steps show you how to use the Font dialog box.

TIP SHEET

▶ **If you like, you can increase the default font size to 12 points so that Word will assume a 12-point instead of 10-point font in future documents you create. In the Font dialog box, set the font to Times New Roman and the font style to Regular. Check to see that Underline is set to none, Color is set to Auto, and none of the Effects check boxes are marked. Select 12-point from the size list, and then click on the Default button. Click on Yes when Word confirms the change, and then click OK to close the Font dialog box.**

▶ **Even though the largest point size in the font-size list boxes is 72, you can print TrueType fonts in even larger sizes. In step 2 or step 6, double-click on the current setting to highlight it, type a larger size (replacing the highlighted number), and press Enter.**

▶ **To change the font size of a single word, you don't need to select it first. Simply click anywhere in the word, then select the desired size from the list in the Formatting toolbar.**

1 Select the text whose size you want to change.

7 Click on the OK button to close the dialog box and apply the new font size to the selected text.

2 Click on the down arrow to the right of the Font Size list in the Formatting toolbar to display the list of font sizes.

3 Scroll if necessary to find the size you want, and then click on it to apply it to the selected text.

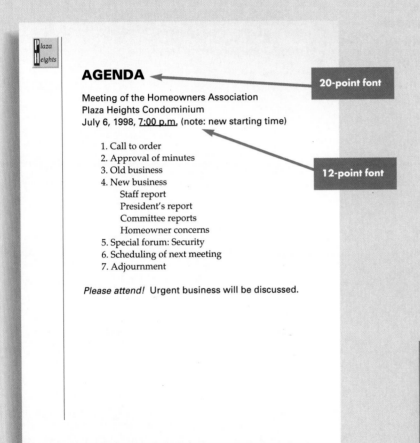

20-point font

12-point font

4 If you want to preview various font sizes, first select the text, and then choose Format, Font to display the Font dialog box.

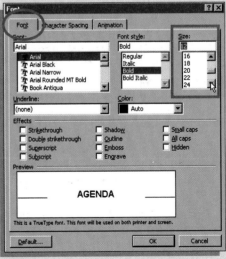

5 Click on the Font tab at the top of the dialog box if it isn't already in front. Then in the Size list, locate the font size you need, scrolling if necessary.

6 Try clicking on a few different sizes; Word displays a sample of the currently selected size in the Preview area at the bottom of the dialog box.

How to Copy Character Formatting

I f you've applied several different character formats—such as a font, a font size, and a font style—to a block of text in your document, and then later decide you'd like to apply the same formatting to another block of text, you don't have to apply those formats one by one to the new location. Instead, you can use the Format Painter button to take all the formats from the original block of text and "paint" them across the new text.

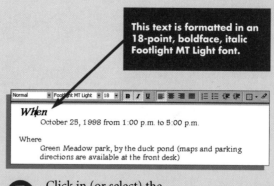

This text is formatted in an 18-point, boldface, italic Footlight MT Light font.

1 Click in (or select) the text that has the formatting you want to copy.

When
October 25, 1998 from 1:00 p.m. to 5:00 p.m.

Where
Green Meadow park, by the duck pond (maps and parking directions are available at the front desk)

Activities
Barbecue, volleyball, horseshoes, games for the kids, and an all-age lawn birds dress up contest

What to Bring
Friends and family (including the four-footed!), a sweater in case it gets breezy, and cold drinks

6 If you want to copy the same formatting across several blocks of text at one time, *double-click* on the Format Painter button in step 2. Word keeps the Format Painter feature turned on so you can drag across multiple blocks of text. For example, you could paint across all the headings in the document shown here. When you're finished, click on the Format Painter button again to turn the feature off.

When
October 25, 1998 from 1:00 p.m. to 5:00 p.m.

Where
Green Meadow park, by the duck pond (maps and parking directions are available at the front desk)

5 Release the mouse. The text takes on the formatting of the original location. You can then click once to deselect the newly formatted text.

2 Click on the Format Painter button in the Standard toolbar.

3 Your mouse pointer changes to an I-beam with an attached paintbrush.

LawnBirds, Inc.

YOU'RE INVITED!
TO LAWNBIRDS' 40TH BIRTHDAY PARTY

When
October 25, 1998 from 1:00 p.m. to 5:00 p.m.

Where
Green Meadow park, by the duck pond (maps and parking directions are available at the front desk)

Activities
Barbecue, volleyball, horseshoes, games for the kids, and an all-age lawn birds dress up contest

What to Bring
Friends and family (including the four-footed!), a sweater in case it gets breezy, and cold drinks

Transportation
Shuttle will pick people up at LawnBirds main entrance at 12:30, 1:00, and 1:30

When
October 25, 1998 from 1:00 p.m. to 5:00 p.m.

Where
Green Meadow park, by the duck pond (maps and parking directions are available at the front desk)

4 Drag across the text to be formatted.

CHAPTER 10

Paragraph Formatting

Paragraph formatting is a broad topic because there are so many formatting features—line spacing, indents, alignment, and so on—that fall into this category. Before you embark on mastering these techniques, you need to understand two key principles.

First, paragraph formatting affects individual paragraphs. If you want to apply paragraph formatting to only one paragraph, you simply place the insertion point in that paragraph before applying the change; Word alters just that paragraph and no others. If you want to apply the change to more than one adjacent paragraph, you have to select the paragraphs first.

Second, Word considers any text followed by a paragraph mark (inserted when you press Enter) to be a paragraph. So a title containing three short lines of text, for example, would contain three separate paragraphs. If you wanted to use the paragraph alignment feature to center the title, you would have to select all three lines (paragraphs) first. By the same token, if you wanted to make an entire document double-spaced, you would have to select the whole document first.

If you find yourself applying certain types of paragraph formatting over and over, read Chapter 13 to learn about styles. Styles make it much easier to apply specific combinations of formatting changes to your text.

How to Change Line Spacing

*L*ine spacing is the amount of space between lines within a paragraph. Word assumes single spacing, which provides just enough space between lines so that letters don't over-lap. Double spacing is good for rough drafts of documents, because it gives you extra room to write in edits by hand. One-and-a-half spacing makes text easier to read by separating lines with an extra half a line of blank space.

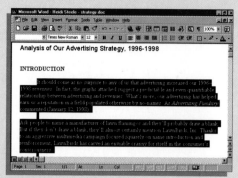

1 If you want to change the line spacing of several adjacent paragraphs, select them first. In the example shown here, all the body text is selected. (If you want to change the line spacing of only one paragraph, see steps 7 and 8.)

TIP SHEET

▶ **For a line spacing other than those offered, skip steps 3 and 4. Instead, in the Paragraph dialog box, click in the At text box (to the right of the Line Spacing list) and type a line-spacing value. For example, type 3 for triple spac-ing. (As soon as you type in the At box, Word changes the Line Spacing setting to Multiple.)**

▶ **A new paragraph takes on the formatting of the preceding one. Therefore, if you are typing in a double-spaced paragraph and you press Enter to start a new paragraph, the new paragraph too will be double-spaced. You can change the line spacing of the new paragraph—or of any para-graph—by following the steps on this page.**

Ask people to name a manufacturer of lawn flamingos and they'll probably draw a blank. But if they don't draw a blank, they'll almost certainly mention LawnBirds, Inc. Thanks to an aggressive multimedia campaign focused squarely on name introduction and reinforcement, LawnBirds has carved an enviable cranny for itself in the consumer's consciousness.

8 The line spacing for this paragraph was changed to one-and-a-half.

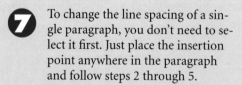

7 To change the line spacing of a sin-gle paragraph, you don't need to se-lect it first. Just place the insertion point anywhere in the paragraph and follow steps 2 through 5.

2 Choose Format, Paragraph to display the Paragraph dialog box.

3 At the top of the Paragraph dialog box, click on the Indents and Spacing tab if it's not already in front. Then display the Line Spacing list by clicking on the down arrow to its right.

awnBirds, Inc.

Analysis of Our Advertising Strategy, 1996–1998

INTRODUCTION

It should come as no surprise to any of us that advertising increased our 1996–1998 revenues. In fact, the graphs attached suggest a predictable and even quantifiable relationship. What's more, our advertising has helped earn us a reputation in a field populated otherwise by no-names. As *Advertising Punditry* commented (January 12, 1998):

Ask people to name a manufacturer of lawn flamingos and they'll probably draw a blank. But if they don't draw a blank, they'll almost certainly mention LawnBirds, Inc. Thanks to an aggressive multimedia campaign focused squarely on name introduction and reinforcement, LawnBirds has carved an enviable cranny for itself in the consumer's consciousness.

The question, then, is not *whether* advertising sells lawn flamingos. It does. The question is *how many* lawn flamingos advertising sells. Do the increased revenues make up our costs? If they have so far, will they continue to? Do the economics call for increasing our ad budget, stabilizing it, decreasing it, or shifting it among the different media?

This analysis attempts to point our advertising in the right direction for the immediate future. However, we must note one obvious constraint: Any hindsight as to what our revenues and profits would have been without advertising is little more than guesswork. The most we can do is project our growth from our preadvertising years and factor in those marketplace changes that we understand and that are quantifiable.

Why did we start advertising in the first place? It's worthwhile occasionally to

Double spacing

One-and-a-half spacing

4 Click on the desired line spacing: Single, 1.5 Lines, or Double.

5 Click on the OK button to close the dialog box.

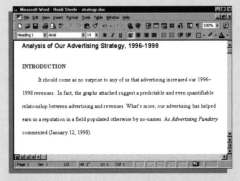

6 The new line spacing is applied to the paragraphs you selected.

How to Indent a Paragraph

Word lets you indent paragraphs from the left margin, the right margin, or both. As with many other features in Word, there is more than one way to indent text. You can use the ruler, the Paragraph dialog box, or the Increase Indent and Decrease Indent buttons on the Formatting toolbar. Try out all three methods to see which one works best for you.

Ask people to name a manufacturer of lawn flamingos and they'll probably draw a blank. But if they don't draw a blank, they'll almost certainly mention LawnBirds, Inc. Thanks to an aggressive multimedia campaign focused squarely on name introduction and reinforcement, LawnBirds has carved an enviable cranny for itself in the consumer's consciousness.

1 Place the insertion point anywhere in the paragraph you want to indent. Alternatively, select adjacent paragraphs to specify the same indentation for all of them.

Increase Indent   **Decrease Indent**

8 You can quickly increase or decrease left indentation one tab stop at a time by clicking the Increase Indent or Decrease Indent button on the Formatting toolbar. (Tab stops are set for every half inch unless you've created custom tabs, as discussed in "How to Set Custom Tabs" later in this chapter.)

7 Click on the OK button to close the dialog box and apply the indentation.

OK

6 At the top of the dialog box, click on the Indents and Spacing tab if it's not already in front. To specify a left indent, double-click in the Left text box to select the existing setting, and type over it with a new amount (in inches). Do the same in the Right text box to add a right indent. You don't need to type the inch sign (").

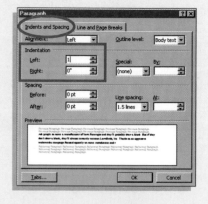

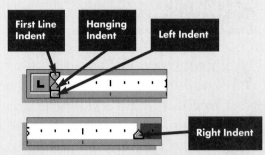

Point to the gray line to display the ruler.

2 This step and the next two describe how to indent text using the ruler. If you don't see the ruler, rest the mouse pointer on the gray horizontal line directly underneath the Formatting toolbar to bring it into view. As soon as you move the mouse pointer off of the ruler, it disappears again. If you want to see the ruler regardless of the position of your mouse pointer, choose View, Ruler. (Repeat this command if you want to hide the ruler.)

First Line Indent · **Hanging Indent** · **Left Indent**

Right Indent

3 To indent a paragraph or selected paragraphs from the left, drag the Left Indent marker (the square). To indent only the first line, drag the First Line Indent marker (the upper triangle). To indent all the lines except the first line (thus creating a hanging indent), drag the Hanging Indent marker (the lower triangle). Finally, to indent a paragraph from the right, drag the Right Indent marker.

LawnBirds, Inc.

Analysis of Our Advertising Strategy, 1996–1998

INTRODUCTION

It should come as no surprise to any of us that advertising increased our 1996–1998 revenues. In fact, the graphs attached suggest a predictable and even quantifiable relationship. What's more, our advertising has helped earn us a reputation in a field populated otherwise by no-names. As *Advertising Punditry* commented (January 12, 1998):

Ask people to name a manufacturer of lawn flamingos and they'll probably draw a blank. But if they don't draw a blank, they'll almost certainly mention LawnBirds, Inc. Thanks to an aggressive multimedia campaign focused squarely on name introduction and reinforcement, LawnBirds has carved an enviable cranny for itself in the consumer's consciousness.

The question, then, is not *whether* advertising sells lawn flamingos. It does. The question is *how many* lawn flamingos advertising sells. Do the increased revenues make up our costs? If they have so far, will they continue to? Do the economics call for increasing our ad budget, stabilizing it, decreasing it, or shifting it among the different media?

This analysis attempts to point our advertising in the right direction for the immediate future. However, we must note one obvious constraint: Any hindsight as to what our revenues and profits would have been without advertising is little more than guesswork. The most we can do is project our growth from our preadvertising years and factor in those marketplace changes that we understand and that are quantifiable.

Why did we start advertising in the first place? It's worthwhile occasionally to remind ourselves why we took the path we took. Recall that in 1991 we saw the

Drag the square to create a left indent.

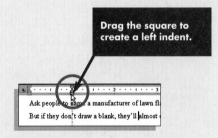

Ask people to name a manufacturer of lawn fl...
But if they don't draw a blank, they'll almost...

4 When the marker is at the desired position on the ruler, release the mouse.

5 To indent text using the Paragraph dialog box, start by choosing Format, Paragraph.

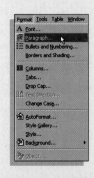

Format Tools Table Window
Font...
Paragraph...
Bullets and Numbering...
Borders and Shading...
Columns...
Tabs...
Drop Cap...
Text Direction...
Change Case...
AutoFormat...
Style Gallery...
Style...
Background...
Object...

How to Change Alignment

lignment refers to the way the right and left edges of a paragraph line up along the margins. By default, Word uses left alignment, which gives paragraphs a straight left edge and a ragged right edge. Occasionally, you may want to justify paragraphs so that both the left and right edges are straight. You usually use centering and right alignment for headings or other short lines of text. On this page, you learn how to change alignment using both the Formatting toolbar and the Paragraph dialog box (although there isn't much advantage to using this longer method).

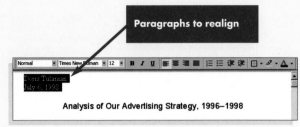

Paragraphs to realign

Analysis of Our Advertising Strategy, 1996–1998

1 Place the insertion point anywhere in the paragraph whose alignment you want to change. Or, select any portion of adjacent paragraphs to specify the same alignment for all of them. In the example shown here, two short paragraphs are selected.

OK

7 Click on the OK button to close the dialog box and apply the alignment.

6 Click on the desired alignment: Left, Centered, Right, or Justified.

TIP SHEET

▸ Indented blocks of text such as the second paragraph in the sample document on this page often look better when they are justified.

▸ When you justify text, Word produces a straight right edge by adding spaces in between the words. If you're justifying narrow blocks of text such as columns or indented paragraphs, you might want to enable hyphenation (Tools, Language, Hyphenation) to even out the length of the lines of text. That way, Word won't have to add much space to shorter lines to justify the right edge, and the gaps between words will be less noticeable.

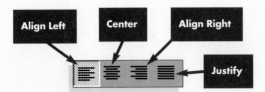

2 Click on one of the four Alignment buttons on the Formatting toolbar: Align Left, Center, Align Right, or Justify. Here, the Align Left button looks "pushed in" because the selected paragraphs are currently left-aligned.

3 Word applies the alignment option you chose to the paragraph or to all of the selected paragraphs.

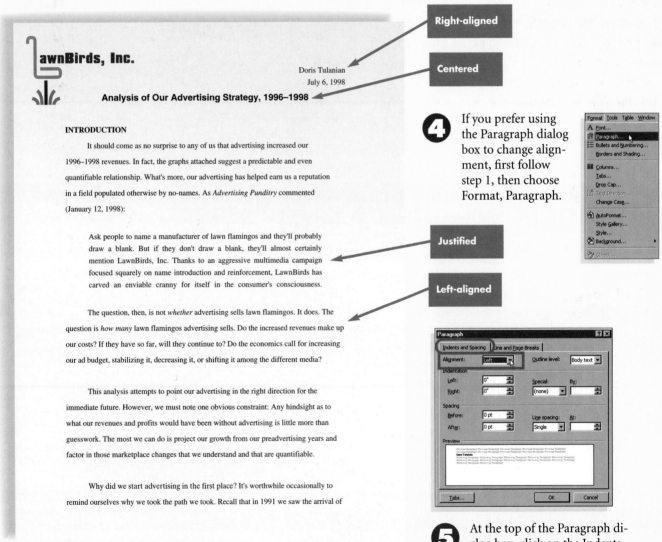

4 If you prefer using the Paragraph dialog box to change alignment, first follow step 1, then choose Format, Paragraph.

5 At the top of the Paragraph dialog box, click on the Indents and Spacing tab if it's not already in front. Then display the Alignment list by clicking on the down arrow to its right.

How to Set Custom Tabs

Word's default tabs are positioned every half inch across the ruler. Each time you press the Tab key, your insertion point moves to the next tab stop, pushing over any text to the right of the insertion point. In regular body text, these default tabs work just fine. When you want to create a list with two or more columns of text, however, it's easier if you replace the default tabs with custom tabs position at the exact locations where you want to line up your text.

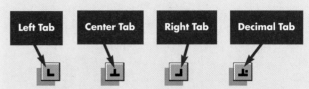

1 You can create four kinds of custom tabs: left, center, right, and decimal. Word uses the symbols shown here to represent the different types. Use left tabs to align text on the left, right tabs to align text on the right, center tabs to center text across the tab, and decimal tabs to align numbers on the decimal point. (See the sample document in the middle of the page for examples of all four types.)

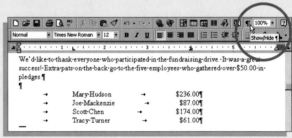

8 When you're working with custom tabs, it's often helpful to click on the Show/Hide button on the Standard toolbar. When Show/Hide is enabled, Word displays arrows to show where you pressed the Tab key and paragraph marks (¶) to show where you pressed Enter.

7 If you decide to shift the position of one of the custom tabs, select all the lines in your list first. Then point to the tab, and drag it along the ruler.

② Click in the paragraph where you want the custom tabs to begin. Before you add any custom tabs, you'll see faint gray tick marks spaced one-half inch apart on the ruler. These are the default tabs. (If you don't see the ruler, see step 2 on the previous page.)

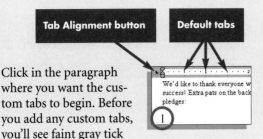

LawnBirds, Inc.

MEMORANDUM

Date: March 10, 1998
To: All Employees
From: Daycare Center Fundraising Committee
Re: Fundraising Drive

We'd like to thank every one who participated in the fundraising drive. It was a great success! Extra pats on the back go to the five employees who gathered over $50.00 in pledges:

Mary Hudson	$236.00
Joe Mackenzie	$87.00
Scott Chen	$174.00
Tracy Turner	$61.00

We'll keep you posted on plans for the next drive. Any ideas or suggestions would be more than welcome. Thanks again for all your hard work.

Here are the final group assignments for the brainstorming sessions discussed in the memo last week:

Group 1	Group 2	Group3
Jan Lao	Travis Jones	Deb Larkin
Marcus Lerner	Elizabeth Montoya	Jefferson Hunter
Sue Johnson	Robin Taylor	Henry Forbes
Pete Chen	Joshua Ng	Pat Smith

③ Use the Tab Alignment button to tell Word which type of custom tab you want to create. When you click on the button repeatedly, you cycle through the symbols representing each of the four tabs. The left tab symbol is showing by default, so you only need to click the Tab Alignment button if you want to create a center, right, or decimal tab. In this example, the column of names is created with a left tab.

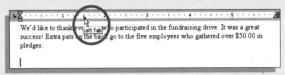

④ Create the custom tab by clicking at the desired position on the ruler. The symbol for the tab appears on the ruler, and all the default tabs to the left of the custom tab disappear.

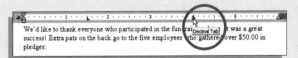

⑤ Repeat steps 3 and 4 to add additional custom tabs if necessary. In this example, a decimal tab is added to the right of the left tab. This tab will be used to line up the dollar amounts in the list.

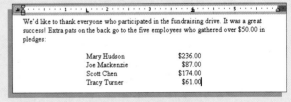

⑥ To use the custom tabs, press the Tab key to move out to the first custom tab stop, and type your text (in this example, an employee name). If you've created another custom tab, press Tab again to move to that tab stop, and type the text (in this example, a dollar amount). Press Enter after typing the last block of text on each line.

How to Create Numbered and Bulleted Lists

Word's numbered and bulleted list features automatically add numbers or bullets when you're typing a list, and they indent the text so that it doesn't wrap underneath the numbers or bullets (see the sample document). What's more, when you type the first item in a list and press Enter, Word automatically turns on the feature for you. (If it doesn't, see the tip on this page.)

▶ **When you cut and paste to change the order of items in a numbered list, Word keeps the numbering sequential. (See Chapter 6 if you need to review how to cut and paste text.)**

▶ **If you want to turn the automatic bulleted lists or automatic numbered lists feature on or off, choose Tools, AutoCorrect, and then click on the AutoFormat As You Type tab. Mark or clear the Automatic Bulleted Lists and Automatic Numbered Lists check boxes, and then click on OK. If you disable these features, you can still turn numbered or bulleted lists on "manually" by clicking on the Numbering or Bullets toolbar buttons.**

▶ **You can change the appearance of the numbers or bullets in your list. Select the list first, then choose Format, Bullets and Numbering, and experiment with the options in the Bullets and Numbering dialog box.**

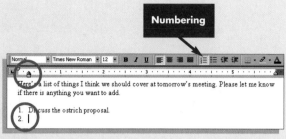

1 To create a numbered list, type **1.** followed by a space, type the text for the first item, and press Enter. Word turns on the numbered list feature (the Numbering button on the Formatting toolbar now looks like it's pushed in), inserts a 2. on the next line, and creates a hanging indent so that the text in items that are more than one line long won't wrap under the number.

7 If you want to separate each item in a list with a blank line, press Shift+Enter, Enter at the end of each item. When you press Shift+Enter, Word inserts a *line break character*, which breaks the line of text without ending the paragraph (thus creating a blank line). Pressing Enter then ends the paragraph and inserts the next number or bullet. (To see where you have pressed Shift+Enter, click on the Show/Hide button on the Standard toolbar. Word represents line break characters with the ↵ symbol.)

6 In this example, the numbered list has been changed to a bulleted list.

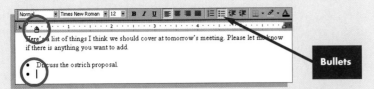

2 To create a bulleted list, type an asterisk (*) followed by a space, type the text for the first item, and then press Enter. Word turns on the bulleted list feature (the Bullets button on the Formatting toolbar looks pushed in); it changes the asterisk to a bullet, inserts another bullet on the next line, and creates a hanging indent.

awnBirds, Inc.

Peter:

Here's a list of things I think we should cover at tomorrow's meeting. Please let me know if there's anything you want to add.

1. Discuss the ostrich proposal.
2. Set a date for the training session. This is important because the consultants are already lined up and waiting for us to finalize the plans.
3. Make a final decision on a new position for the department.
4. Review the report on customer satisfaction. It's about time we put the less than satisfactory results of the customer survey out on the table.
5. Eat bagels and drink good coffee!

Talk to you soon,

JoAnne

3 Continue typing items, pressing Enter at the end of each one.

4 After you type the last item, press Enter twice to turn the numbered or bulleted list feature off.

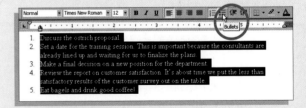

5 If you want to change the numbers to bullets (or vice versa), select the entire list, and then click on the Bullets or Numbering button on the Formatting toolbar.

How to Add Borders and Shading

You don't have to know anything about graphics to add attractive borders and shading to headings and paragraphs of body text, and you can even create a decorative border around the entire page. The steps on this page tell you how to work with the Borders and Shading dialog box. However, you can also issue most of the commands with the Tables and Borders toolbar (choose View, Toolbars, Tables and Borders).

1 Click in the paragraph to which you want to add borders and shading, or select adjacent paragraphs if you want to add borders and shading to all of them.

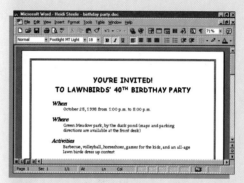

9 Word creates the border around every page in your document.

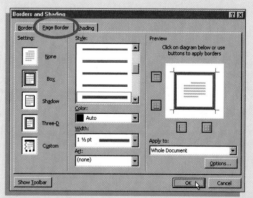

8 To create a border around your page, click on the Page Border tab in the Borders and Shading dialog box, specify the type of border you want, and click on OK.

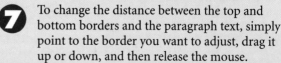

7 To change the distance between the top and bottom borders and the paragraph text, simply point to the border you want to adjust, drag it up or down, and then release the mouse.

2 Choose Format, Borders and Shading to display the Borders and Shading dialog box.

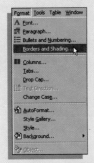

3 Click on the Borders tab if it isn't already in front. If you see an option under Setting that closely matches the type of border you want to add, click on it.

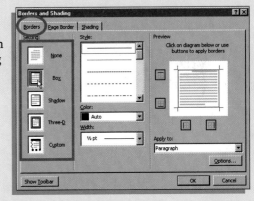

LawnBirds, Inc.

MEMORANDUM

Date: March 10, 1998
To: All Employees
From: Daycare Center Fundraising Committee
Re: Fundraising Drive

We'd like to thank every one who participated in the fundraising drive. It was a great success! Extra pats on the back go to the five employees who gathered over $50.00 in pledges:

Mary Hudson	$236.00
Joe Mackenzie	$87.00
Scott Chen	$174.00
Tracy Turner	$61.00

We'll keep you posted on plans for the next drive. Any ideas or suggestions would be more than welcome. Thanks again for all your hard work.

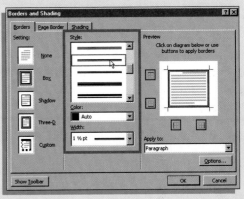

4 To customize the style of the lines in your border, scroll through the Style list, and click on the desired style. You can also use the Color and Width drop-down lists to change the color and width of the lines. If you want to design a border "from scratch," choose Custom under Setting, select the desired style, color, and width options for one of the lines, and then click on the line in the sample box under Preview. Repeat this process to create the remaining three lines.

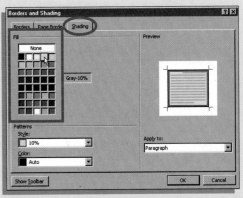

OK

6 When you've made all of your selections in the Borders and Shading dialog box, click on the OK button.

5 To add shading, click on the Shading tab at the top of the dialog box, and then click on the desired color under Fill.

CHAPTER 11

Page Formatting

In this chapter, the last of three on formatting, you explore Word's most useful page formatting features. You learn how to change margins, how to begin a new page where you want to rather than where Word decides to, how to tell Word what size paper you are printing on, and how to center text vertically on the page.

Unlike character and paragraph formatting, page formatting by default affects every page of the document, not just certain characters or paragraphs. Consequently, it doesn't matter where your insertion point is when you make a change to the page formatting, and you shouldn't select any text first.

Most of the time, you want page formatting to affect the entire document. Once in a while, however, you may need to apply different page formatting to different portions of the same document. (For example, you may need to vertically center the title page of a report, but not the other pages in the document.) To do this, you have to insert *section breaks* to divide the document into two or more sections. You can then apply different page formatting to each separate section of the document. Section breaks are discussed in "How to Control Page Breaks" and "How to Center Text Vertically on the Page" in this chapter, and in "How to Create Columns" in Chapter 15.

How to Change the Page Margins

Word's default margins are 1 inch on the top and bottom of the page and 1.25 inches on the left and right. These margins are fine for most documents, but like all features in Word, they are by no means mandatory. Larger margins can give the page a more spacious feel, and narrower margins can come in handy when you're trying to fit text onto one page. For example, in the document on this page, all the introductory text of a business report fits on one page thanks to some rather narrow margins.

TIP SHEET

▸ If you want to see what the margins will look like before you print, use Print Preview or Page Layout view (see Chapters 2 and 4).

▸ Rather than type a margin setting in steps 4 and 5, you can click on the up and down arrows next to the text boxes to adjust the setting in increments of one-tenth of an inch.

▸ If your company uses margin settings on all its documents that differ from Word's default margins, you can set the default margins to match those used by your company. This way, you won't have to change the margins each time you start a new document. To do this, follow steps 1 through 5 on this page, but before you click on the OK button in step 6, click on the Default button. Word asks if you want to change the default settings for page setup. Click on the Yes button, then click on OK. If you later want to change the default margins to something else, just repeat these steps.

1 Choose File, Page Setup. (It doesn't matter where the insertion point is resting, and you shouldn't have any text selected.)

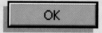

6 Click on the OK button to close the dialog box and apply the change.

5 Change any other margins you want to reset.

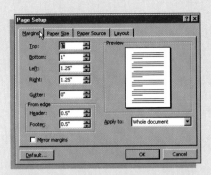

2 In the Page Setup dialog box, click on the Margins tab if it is not already active.

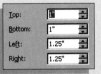

3 The contents of the Top text box is selected when the dialog box is first displayed. If you want to change the top margin first, go on to the next step. To begin with the bottom, left, or right margin, first select the existing setting in the appropriate text box by double-clicking on it or by pressing the Tab key to move to it.

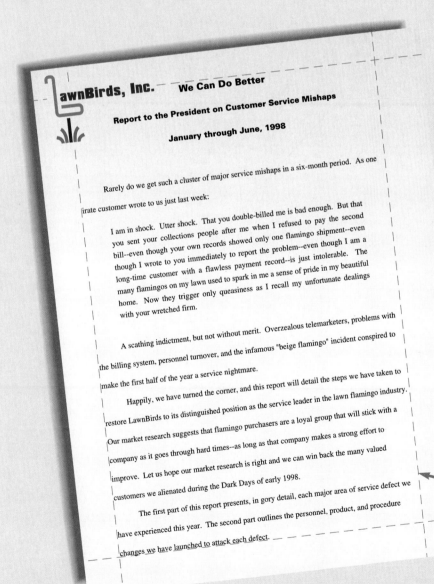

LawnBirds, Inc.   We Can Do Better

Report to the President on Customer Service Mishaps

January through June, 1998

Rarely do we get such a cluster of major service mishaps in a six-month period. As one irate customer wrote to us just last week:

I am in shock. Utter shock. That you double-billed me is bad enough. But that you sent your collections people after me when I refused to pay the second bill--even though your own records showed only one flamingo shipment--even though I wrote to you immediately to report the problem--even though I am a long-time customer with a flawless payment record--is just intolerable. The many flamingos on my lawn used to spark in me a sense of pride in my beautiful home. Now they trigger only queasiness as I recall my unfortunate dealings with your wretched firm.

A scathing indictment, but not without merit. Overzealous telemarketers, problems with the billing system, personnel turnover, and the infamous "beige flamingo" incident conspired to make the first half of the year a service nightmare.

Happily, we have turned the corner, and this report will detail the steps we have taken to restore LawnBirds to its distinguished position as the service leader in the lawn flamingo industry. Our market research suggests that flamingo purchasers are a loyal group that will stick with a company as it goes through hard times--as long as that company makes a strong effort to improve. Let us hope our market research is right and we can win back the many valued customers we alienated during the Dark Days of early 1998.

The first part of this report presents, in gory detail, each major area of service defect we have experienced this year. The second part outlines the personnel, product, and procedure changes we have launched to attack each defect.

4 Type a new setting in inches. (Typing the inch symbol is optional.) The number you type replaces the existing setting.

Narrow margins help fit all the text on one page.

How to Control Page Breaks

As you type a multiple-page document, Word ends each page when it's full by inserting *soft page breaks* (also called *automatic page breaks*), which are displayed on screen as horizontal dotted lines. As you add or delete text, Word adjusts the position of soft page breaks accordingly. Occasionally, you may need to insert a *hard page break* (also called a *manual page break*) to force a page to break before it is full. You could, for example, insert a hard page break to force a new section of a report to begin at the top of the next page, or to separate a title page from the remainder of a document.

TIP SHEET

▶ It's best to add hard page breaks after you've finished editing a document, because if you add or delete text in a document that contains hard page breaks you will probably end up shoving the breaks into the wrong places. If you do edit a document with existing hard page breaks, be prepared to delete them (and possibly add others elsewhere).

▶ If you want to vertically center the title on the first page of a report, you need to insert a *section break* instead of a hard page break between the title page and the next page. Instead of pressing Ctrl+Enter as in step 2, choose Insert, Break to display the Break dialog box. Under Section Breaks, click on the Next Page option button, then click on OK to insert a *next page* section break (displayed as a dotted double line with the words *Section Break (Next Page) Section* on it). This type of break both starts a new section and breaks the page. You can now follow the steps in "How to Center Text Vertically on the Page" later in this chapter to center the title.

1 Place the insertion point where you want the page to break.

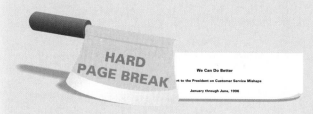

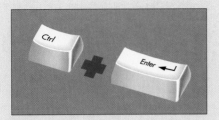

2 Press Ctrl+Enter. (Hold down the Ctrl key and press Enter.)

January through June, 1998

┄┄┄┄┄┄┄┄┄┄ Page Break ┄┄┄┄┄┄┄┄┄┄

Rarely do we get such a cluster of major service mishaps in a six-month period.

As one irate customer wrote to us just last week:

---

3 Word inserts a hard page break at the insertion point. Assuming you're using Normal view, the page break appears as a dotted horizontal line with the words *Page Break* on it. In Page Layout view, you see a separation between the two pages. (To review how to change views, see Chapter 4.)

LawnBirds, Inc.

Rarely do we get such a cluster
irate customer wrote to us just last we

I am in shock. Utter
you sent your collect
even though your o
I wrote to you imm
customer with a fl
on my lawn used
trigger only que
firm.

A scathing indictmen
the billing system, personne
make the first half of the y

Happily, we have
restore LawnBirds to its
Our market research s
company as it goes th
improve. Let us ho
customers we alier

The first p
have experience
changes we ha

LawnBirds, Inc.

vice mishaps in a six-month period. As one

We Can Do Better

Report to the President on Customer Service Mishaps

January through June, 1998

┄┄┄┄┄┄┄┄┄┄ Page Break ┄┄┄┄┄┄┄┄┄┄

Rarely do we get such a cluster of major s

As one irate customer wrote to us just last week:

---

4 To delete a hard page break, place the insertion point on the break and press the Delete key. Or, if your insertion point is positioned directly underneath the page break (as shown in step 3), you can press the Backspace key to delete it.

How to Change the Paper Size

Word assumes you want to use 8.5-by-11-inch paper unless you tell it otherwise. If you are planning to print a document on paper of a different size, you need to tell Word the dimensions of the paper so that it can adjust line and page breaks for you.

▶ **1** Choose File, Page Setup. (Your insertion point can be anywhere in the document, and you should not have any text selected.)

▶ **Before printing the document, be sure to make the alternate paper available to your printer. (Exactly how you do this varies by printer.) If your printer has more than one paper tray, you may also have to tell Word where to find the new paper. To do this, click on the Paper Source tab in the Page Setup dialog box and make the appropriate selections in the First Page and Other Pages lists.**

▶ **If necessary, you can change the orientation of your paper. Normally, the page is oriented vertically—this is known as *portrait* mode. To orient the page horizontally so that the text prints out across the length of the page, switch to *landscape* mode by clicking on the Landscape option button in the Paper Size tab of the Page Setup dialog box (see the figure in step 2).**

7 Word adjusts line breaks and soft page breaks (if any) to account for the new dimensions of the page.

6 Click on the OK button to close the dialog box and apply the change.

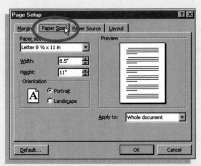

2 In the Page Setup dialog box, click on the Paper Size tab if it is not already active.

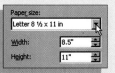

3 Click on the arrow to the right of the Paper Size box.

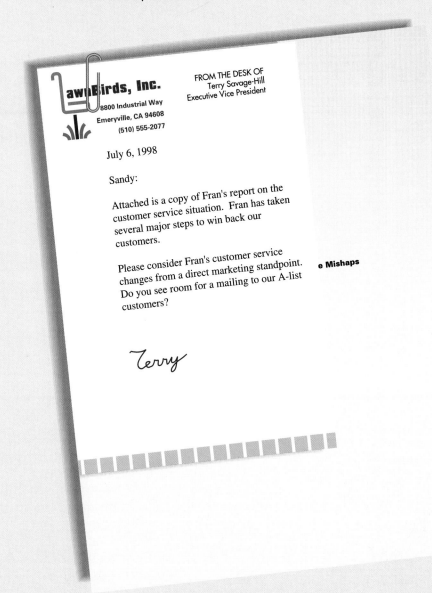

4 A list of predefined paper sizes drops down. If you see the size you want to use, click on it and skip to step 6. Otherwise, click on Custom Size and proceed to step 5.

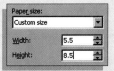

5 To define a custom size, double-click in the Width text box to select the existing setting, and type a new width for the paper in inches. Then press Tab or double-click in the Height text box, and type the height in inches. (You don't have to type the inch symbol.)

How to Center Text Vertically on the Page

If you are like many other beginning Word users, you may have tried to vertically center a short letter or title by pressing Enter several times at the beginning of the text to force it down the page. More often than not, you end up pressing Enter too many (or too few) times and then have to add or delete blank lines to get the text aligned correctly. A much easier method is to let Word vertically center the text for you.

▶**❶** If you want to vertically center a one-page document, skip to the next step. If you want to vertically center the title page of a multiple-page document, delete the existing hard page break separating the title page from the rest of the pages, and replace it with a *next page section break.* For help with this, see the Tip Sheet in "How to Control Page Breaks" earlier in this chapter.

❼ Click on the OK button to close the dialog box and apply the change.

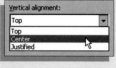

❻ Click on Center.

Remove any blank lines above and below the text.

2 Remove any blank lines from above and below the text you want to center vertically. (You can click on the Show/Hide button in the Standard toolbar to easily check whether you have blank lines.) Leave the insertion point in the page, and don't select any text.

3 Choose File, Page Setup to display the Page Setup dialog box.

Text is centered vertically on the page.

4 Click on the Layout tab if it isn't already active.

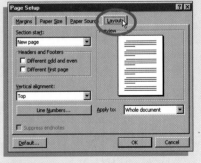

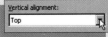

5 Click on the down arrow to the right of the Vertical Alignment box to drop down the list of options.

TRY IT!

Here is a chance to sharpen the formatting skills you've acquired in the last three chapters. Follow these steps to type and format the two-page document pictured below. As you follow this exercise, keep in mind that the line breaks in your paragraphs will not necessarily match those shown here, because the lines in some of the figures were shortened to make the text easier to read.

1

Start a new document and save it as Plaza. If your ruler is not already displayed, choose View, Ruler to bring it into view.

Pool and Recreation Area
Plaza Heights Condominium
published June 6, 1997

Section 3.A.7 of our bylaws states:

Use of the swimming pool and recreation area is for owners, residents, and their accompanied guests only. No person may use the pool or recreation area in such a way that interferes with any other person's enjoyment of these areas or of any residence. The Board of Directors may from time to time publish and amend specific rules in the furtherance of this bylaw.

In the spirit of our bylaws, we publish the following amended rules:

1. The area is open every day from 6:00 a.m. to 10:00 p.m.

2. No food or drink is allowed except in the deck area.

3. Shirt and shoes must be worn to and from the recreation area.

4. Children under 12 must be accompanied by an adult.

5. An owner or resident may have no more than four guests in the area at one time. Guests must be accompanied by an owner or resident at all times.

2

Type the three lines shown here, and press Enter once.

Pool and Recreation Area
Plaza Heights Condominium
Published June 6, 1997

5

Click any-where in the three lines of text, and then choose File, Page Setup.

3

Choose Insert, Break to display the Break dialog box.

6

Click on the Layout tab if it isn't already in front, and click on the down arrow to the right of the Vertical Alignment box.

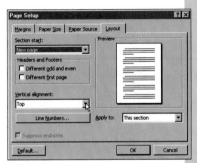

4

Click on the Next Page radio button under Section Breaks, and then click on OK to insert a next page section break.

7

Click on the Center op-tion, and then click on the OK button.

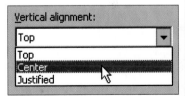

Continue to next page ▶

**Continue
below**

Select the
three lines you typed (but not the section break).

Make the following selections in the
Formatting toolbar: Arial font (if available); 14-point font size; bold.

With the three lines still selected, click
on the Center button in the Formatting
toolbar.

11

At the end of
the docu-
ment, type
the next three
paragraphs as
shown here,
pressing Enter twice between paragraphs and at the end of the last paragraph to add blank line.

12

Select the first paragraph you just
typed (*Section 3.A.7...*).

13

In the Formatting toolbar, drop down
the Font Size list and choose 12-point,
then click on the Italic button.

14

With the text still selected, click on the
Format Painter button in the
Formatting toolbar.

Drag the paint-brush mouse pointer across the last paragraph of the document (*In the spirit...*), and then release the mouse button to copy the formatting from the first paragraph.

 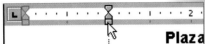

Place the insertion point anywhere in the next-to-last paragraph (*Use of the...*). In the ruler, drag the Left Indent marker (the small square) to the 1-inch mark, and release the mouse.

At the end of the document, type **1.**, followed by a space, then type the first pool and recreation area rule shown here, and press Enter. Word automatically inserts a 2. for you on the next line.

Type the remaining four rules shown here, and press Enter twice at the end of the last rule to turn off automatic numbering.

Select the five rules you just typed, and then change the font size to 12-point and click on the Bold button on the Formatting toolbar.

 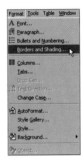

Keep the text selected, and choose Format, Borders and Shading to display the Borders and Shading dialog box.

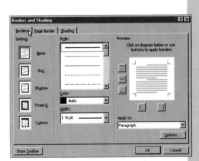

In the Borders and Shading dialog box, click on the Borders tab if it isn't already in front.

Continue to next page ▶

TRY IT!

Continue below

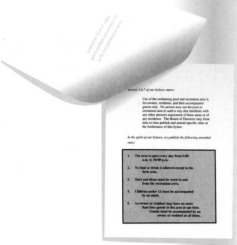

24

In the Fill area, click on the Gray-10% square in the color palette.

22

Click on the Box option under Setting.

25

Click on the OK button to close the Borders and Shading dialog box.

23

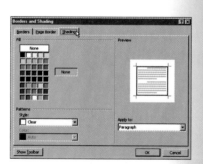

Click on the Shading tab in the Borders and Shading dialog box.

26

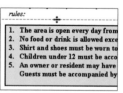

Deselect the text by clicking any-
where. Then drag the bottom border (below the fifth rule) down approxi-mately one-quarter inch to increase the distance between the text and the bor-der, and do the same with the top bor-der, dragging upward the same distance.

27

Choose File, Page Setup to display the Page Setup dialog box.

28

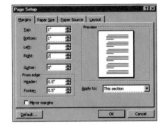

Click on the Margins tab if it is not already active. In the Left text box, type 2 for a 2-inch left margin. In the Right text box, specify a 2-inch right margin as well. Then click on OK.

29

Select the whole document, and then choose Format, Paragraph.

30

Click on the Indents and Spacing tab if it isn't already in front. In the Line Spacing list, select 1.5 Lines. Then click on the OK button.

31

Click anywhere in the excerpt from the condominium bylaws (*Use of the...*), choose Format, Paragraph, and specify single spacing.

32

Check your spelling, resave the document, print it, and close it.

CHAPTER 12

How to Work with Long Documents

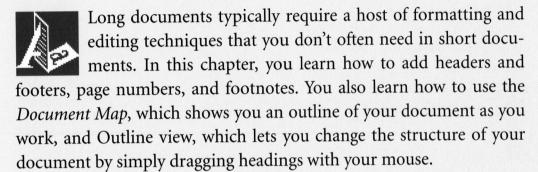Long documents typically require a host of formatting and editing techniques that you don't often need in short documents. In this chapter, you learn how to add headers and footers, page numbers, and footnotes. You also learn how to use the *Document Map*, which shows you an outline of your document as you work, and Outline view, which lets you change the structure of your document by simply dragging headings with your mouse.

A *header* is text that prints at the top of every page, and a *footer* is text that prints at the bottom of every page. You can use headers and footers for information such as the page number, the date, your name, the name of your organization, and so on.

Page numbering is an essential topic for anyone who creates documents that are longer than a page or two. The technique for adding page numbers described in this chapter makes use of headers and footers, so you should read these first two topics in sequence.

If you have to prepare reports or write papers, chances are you need to use footnotes. Word's footnote feature places and numbers footnotes for you. You don't have to worry about leaving room at the bottom of the page or renumbering footnotes if you add one early in the document.

Word's Document Map and Outline view require that you first apply *styles* or *outline levels* to your headings. If these two outlining features look intriguing to you, then jump ahead to Chapter 13 to learn how to apply styles and outline levels, and then come back to explore these two topics in more depth.

How to Type Headers and Footers

A header appears at the top of every page, and a footer appears at the bottom of every page. You might want to use headers and footers to display the document title, your name, the name of your organization, and so on. You can also place fields in headers and footers. (A *field* is a holding place for information that Word updates automatically, such as the current date.) Finally, Word offers several AutoText entries specially designed for headers and footers.

TIP SHEET

▶ If you need to delete a field in a header or footer, first select it and then press Delete. When you click on a field, it turns a light shade of gray. The field isn't actually selected, however, until you double-click on it or drag across it with the mouse.

▶ If you want different headers or footers on odd and even pages of your document (this is common for documents that will be bound), choose File, Page Setup, click on the Layout tab, mark the Different Odd and Even check box, and click on OK. You can then use the Show Next and Show Previous buttons in the Header and Footer toolbar to navigate between the headers and footers for odd and even pages.

▶ If you want different headers and footers in different portions of your document, insert *next page section breaks* to divide your document into two or more sections. (See the Tip Sheet in "How to Control Page Breaks" in Chapter 11). By default, Word carries the same header and footer across all sections of your document. To allow the headers and footers to vary, click in each section, and click on the Same As Previous button in the Header and Footer toolbar to turn off the feature. You can use the Show Next and Show Previous buttons in the toolbar to display the header and footer areas for each different section.

1 Choose View, Header and Footer. It doesn't matter where the insertion point is resting because headers and footers automatically appear on every page. (If you don't want to print the header and/or footer on the first page of your document, follow steps 6 and 7 on the next page.)

8 Click on the Close button in the Header and Footer toolbar to return to viewing the document text. Headers and footers aren't visible in Normal view, but you can see them in both Page Layout view and in Print Preview. (In fact, you can activate the header and footer areas from Page Layout view by simply double-clicking on them.)

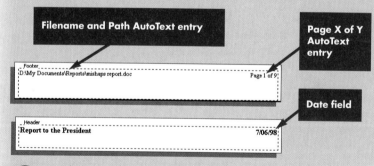

7 In this example, the header includes regular text on the left margin, and the date field on the right. The footer contains two AutoText entries, Filename and Path on the left, and Page X of Y on the right. After you've typed your text (and inserted any fields or AutoText entries), you can select it and format it in the usual ways. For example, you may want to decrease the font size to make the header and footer text less prominent.

Footer area

Header area

Header and Footer toolbar

2 Word switches to Page Layout view, places the insertion point in the header area, and displays the Header and Footer toolbar, which contains buttons that access special commands for working with headers and footers.

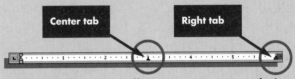

Switch Between Header and Footer

3 If you want to type a footer, click on the Switch Between Header and Footer button to place the insertion point in the footer area. You can go back to the header area by clicking on this button again.

Center tab   **Right tab**

4 Word automatically creates two custom tabs in the header and footer areas: one center tab in the middle of the page, and one right tab at the right margin. These tabs make it simple to align your text. To enter text on the left, just start typing when your insertion point is still at the left margin. To center the text, press Tab once to move to the center tab, and start typing. To align text on the right margin, press Tab twice before typing.

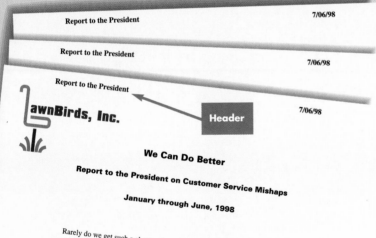

Header

Footer

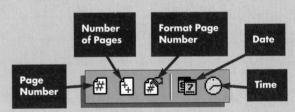

Number of Pages   **Format Page Number**   **Date**

Page Number   **Time**

5 Click on the Date and Time toolbar buttons to insert fields for the current date and time. Click on the Page Number button to insert the page number, and the Number of Pages button to insert the total number of pages. See the Tip Sheet on the next page for information about the Format Page Number button.

6 Clicking on the Insert AutoText button in the Header and Footer toolbar displays a list of AutoText entries. Most of them insert a combination of text and fields. The first entry inserts the page number surrounded by dashes (-1-). The second and third entries use commas to show you where the text will be placed—on the left margin, in the center of the page, or on the right margin. If you insert an entry you don't want to keep, select it and press the Delete key.

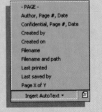

How to Add Page Numbers

Word offers two methods for adding page numbers to your document. You can use the Insert, Page Numbers command to tell Word what type of page number you want and where it should appear. Word then adds the page number field to the header or footer for you. Given that you already know how to work with headers and footers, however, you'll probably find it easier to insert the field yourself. This way, you can enter any other text you might want in the header or footer at the same time, and you have more control over the formatting. If you haven't yet read "How to Type Headers and Footers" on the previous page, do so now before following the steps on this page.

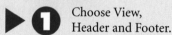

▶ 1 Choose View, Header and Footer.

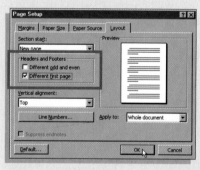

7 Click on the Layout tab if it isn't already active, mark the Different First Page check box under Headers and Footers, and click on OK.

6 If you don't want the page number (or other header/footer text) to appear on the first page of your document, choose File, Page Setup.

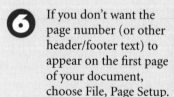

2 If you want the page number to go at the bottom of the page, click the Switch Between Header and Footer button in the Header and Footer toolbar to display the footer area.

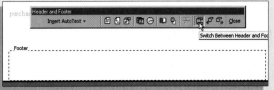

3 If you want the page number centered in the middle of the page, press Tab once. If you want it to be right-aligned, press Tab twice. Optionally, you can type the word *Page* followed by a space, so that your page numbers will appear as *Page 1*, *Page 2*, and so on. Click the Page Number button on the Header and Footer toolbar to insert the page number field. (You can also click on the Number of Pages button if you need to insert the total number of pages.)

7/06/98

Report to the President

awnBirds, Inc.

We Can Do Better

Report to the President on Customer Service Mishaps

January through June, 1998

Rarely do we get such a cluster of major service mishaps in a six-month period. As one irate customer wrote to us just last week:

I am in shock. Utter shock. That you double-billed me is bad enough. But that you sent your collections people after me when I refused to pay the second bill--even though your own records showed only one flamingo shipment--even though I wrote to you immediately to report the problem-- even though I am a long-time customer with a flawless payment record--is just intolerable. The many flamingos on my lawn used to spark in me a sense of pride in my beautiful home. Now they trigger only queasiness as I recall my unfortunate dealings with your wretched firm.

A scathing indictment, but not without merit. Overzealous telemarketers, problems with the billing system, personnel turnover, and the infamous "beige flamingo" incident conspired to make the first half of the year a service nightmare.

Happily, we have turned the corner, and this report will detail the steps we have taken to restore LawnBirds to its distinguished position as the service leader in the lawn flamingo industry. Our market research suggests that flamingo purchasers are a loyal group that will stick with a company as it goes through hard times--as long as that company makes a strong effort to improve. Let us hope our market research is right and

Page 1

Page 2

Page 3

Page number field

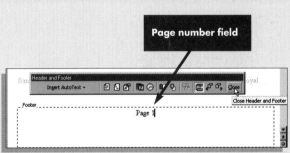

4 Add any other header or footer text you'd like, format it if desired, and click the Close button on the Header and Footer toolbar to return to Normal view.

These AutoText entries include the page number.

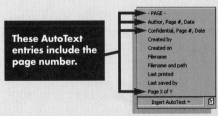

5 Optionally, you can use one of four AutoText entries that include the page number. Click on the Insert AutoText button to display the list shown here, and click on the desired option.

How to Type Footnotes

To add a footnote in Word, you just specify where the footnote should be referenced in the document and what it should contain. Word makes sure that the numbering is accurate—no matter how many notes you add, delete, or move—and that the note always appears on the same page as its reference. The steps on this page assume you are working in Normal view. See the Tip Sheet for information on creating footnotes in Page Layout view.

1 Place the insertion point where you want the footnote reference to appear.

TIP SHEET

▶ **To edit or reformat a footnote from Normal view, double-click on the reference mark for the footnote in the document. Word opens the footnote pane, which displays all of your document's footnotes one after the other. When you are finished, click on the Close button at the top of the footer pane. If you are in Page Layout view, you can simply scroll the footnote into view and edit or reformat it as you would ordinary document text.**

▶ **To delete a footnote, select its reference mark in the document and press Delete.**

▶ **You can move a footnote reference mark the same way you move any character (see Chapter 6). If you move it to a new page, the footnote text moves to the new page with it.**

7 To read a footnote, simply rest the mouse pointer over its reference mark. In a moment, a ScreenTip appears with the footnote text. When you're done reading the text, click once to hide it.

6 Click on the Close button at the top of the footnote pane to close it.

2 Choose Insert, Footnote to display the Footnote and Endnote dialog box.

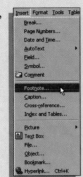

3 Make sure the Footnote and AutoNumber option buttons are marked, as they are by default. (Note that you can create endnotes instead of footnotes, if you prefer.) Click on OK to close the dialog box.

7/06/98

Report to the President

LawnBirds, Inc.

We Can Do Better

Report to the President on Customer Service Mishaps

January through June, 1998

Rarely do we get such a cluster of major service mishaps in a six-month period. As one irate customer wrote to us just last week:

I am in shock. Utter shock. That you double-billed me is bad enough. But that you sent your collections people after me when I refused to pay the second bill--even though your own records showed only one flamingo shipment--even though I wrote to you immediately to report the problem-- even though I am a long-time customer with a flawless payment record--is just intolerable. The many flamingos on my lawn used to spark in me a sense of pride in my beautiful home. Now they trigger only queasiness as I recall my unfortunate dealings with your wretched firm.[1]

A scathing indictment, but not without merit. Overzealous telemarketers, problems with the billing system, personnel turnover, and the infamous "beige flamingo" incident[2] conspired to make the first half of the year a service nightmare.

Happily, we have turned the corner, and this report will detail the steps we have

[1] Letter from customer Victoria Rynar, dated June 2, 1998. Original on file along with our response, dated June 9, 1998.

[2] In the "beige flamingo" incident, several hundred flamingos were produced with defective coloring that faded to beige after the first rainfall.

Page 1

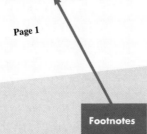

Footnotes

Reference mark   **Footnote pane**

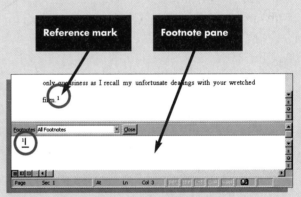

4 A footnote pane appears at the bottom of the document window and Word inserts a footnote reference mark, both in the document and in the footnote pane.

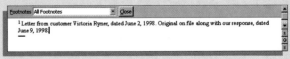

5 Type and format the footnote text just as you would ordinary document text. There is no length limit for footnotes, but Word may have to continue a long note on the next page because it doesn't let footnotes take up more than half the page.

How to Use the Document Map

The Document Map gives you a bird's-eye view of your headings as you're working. It shows you where you are in a long document, and you can use it to quickly jump from section to section. The Document Map works best if you format your headings with heading styles, as shown in the examples on this page, or outline levels. (See Chapter 13 to learn how apply this formatting). If Word doesn't find heading styles or outline levels, it searches for paragraphs that look like headings (for example, short lines formatted in a larger font size), applies outline levels to them, and then displays them in the Document Map.

▶ **1** Click on the Document Map button in the Standard toolbar.

8 To adjust the width of the Document Map pane, point to the boundary between the Document Map and the document, and when you see the Resize ScreenTip, drag to the desired spot and release the mouse. To close the Document Map, either double-click on the boundary or click on the Document Map button on the Standard toolbar again.

7 In this example, clicking on Heading 2 in the context menu collapsed the Document Map to display only headings formatted with the Heading 1 and Heading 2 styles.

TIP SHEET

▶ If the Document Map is blank, it means that Word couldn't find any paragraphs formatted with heading styles or outline levels, or paragraphs that looked like headings. If this happens, follow the directions in the first two topics of the next chapter to apply heading styles or outline levels to your headings, and then redisplay the Document Map.

▶ If you need to change the levels of some of your headings or move headings around in your document, use Outline view instead of the Document Map (see the next page).

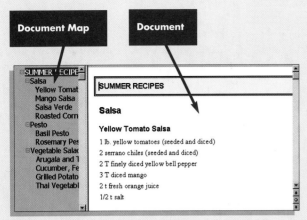

2 Word opens the Document Map on the left side of the document window, and it uses indentation to show the levels of the various headings in the outline. In this example, the heading SUMMER RECIPES (formatted with the Heading 1 style) contains three subheadings, Salsa, Pesto, and Vegetable Salad (formatted with the Heading 2 style), which in turn contain subheadings for the individual recipes (formatted with the Heading 3 style).

3 To move to a particular heading in your document, click on the heading in the Document Map. If the heading is wider than the Document Map pane, Word displays a ScreenTip containing the entire heading when you point to it.

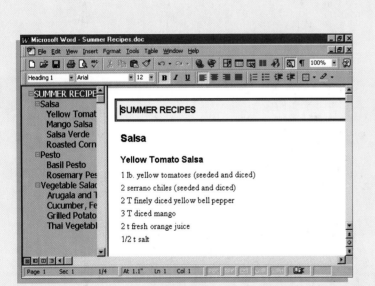

4 In this example, clicking on the Roasted Corn and Tomato Salsa heading in the previous step instantly brought that section of the document into view.

6 If you want to expand or collapse the view of the entire Document Map, right-click anywhere in the Document Map to display the context menu shown here, and click on the deepest heading level you want to view.

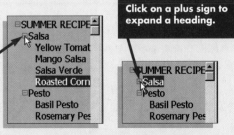

5 You can expand or collapse the view of headings that contain subheadings in the Document Map. Clicking on a minus sign hides all the subheadings, and clicking on a plus sign displays them.

How to Use Outline View

Outline view is similar to the Document Map, but it's intended to help you modify the structure of your outline instead of simply helping you navigate. In Outline view, you can move headings—and any body text or sub-headings they contain—using drag-and-drop, and you can adjust heading levels by clicking on toolbar buttons. You have to apply heading styles or outline levels to your headings before using Outline view (see Chapter 13).

1 Choose View, Outline (or click on the Outline View button in the lower-left corner of the document window).

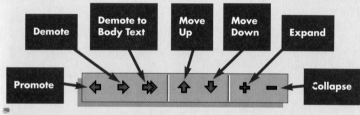

8 If you want to promote a heading to a higher level or demote it to a lower level, select the heading, and then click on the Promote, Demote, and Demote to Body Text buttons. When you change the level of a heading, Word adjusts the level of all its subheadings accordingly.

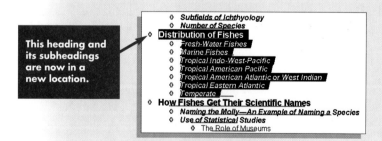

This heading and its subheadings are now in a new location.

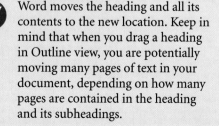

7 Word moves the heading and all its contents to the new location. Keep in mind that when you drag a heading in Outline view, you are potentially moving many pages of text in your document, depending on how many pages are contained in the heading and its subheadings.

2 Word switches to Outline view (see the figure in the middle of the page) and displays the Outlining toolbar.

3 You can expand or collapse the outline by clicking on the toolbar buttons containing the numbers 1 through 7. Click on the All button to display the entire document, both headings and body text.

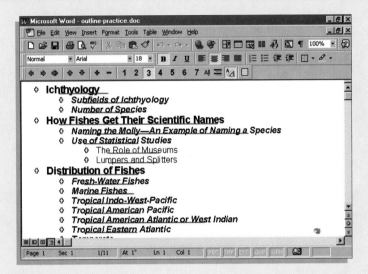

4 In this example, clicking on the 1 button in the previous step collapsed the outline to show only headings formatted with the Heading 1 style.

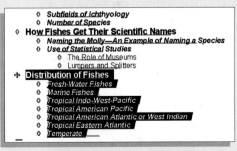

5 To move a heading (along with its subheadings and body text) to a new location in the document, first select the heading (and any subheadings) by clicking on the plus sign next to it. When you point to the plus sign, the mouse pointer changes shape to become a four-headed arrow.

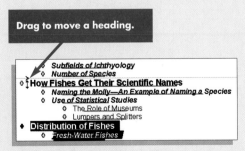

6 Drag up or down in the outline. As you a drag, the mouse pointer becomes a double arrow, and a faint horizontal line with a small black arrow indicates where the heading will move. When the line is in the right location, release the mouse.

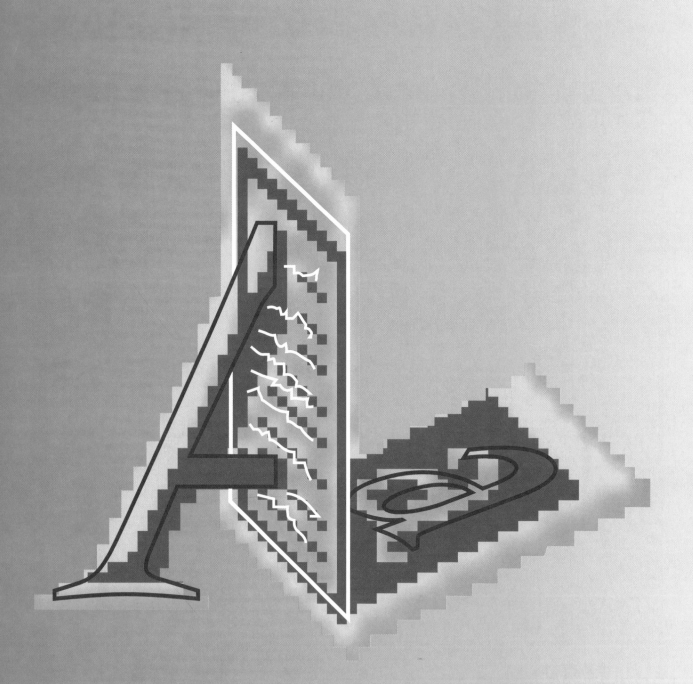

CHAPTER 13

Using Styles and Outline Levels

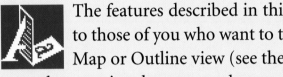The features described in this chapter will have great appeal to those of you who want to take advantage of the Document Map or Outline view (see the previous chapter) or who need to apply extensive character and paragraph formatting in documents.

If you only want to use the Document Map and Outline view and don't need to learn shortcuts for applying and modifying formatting codes, you need only read the first topic, "How to Apply Outline Levels."

If, on the other hand, you want save time when formatting, you should explore the last three topics of the chapter, which discuss styles. A *style* is a collection of formatting codes to which you have assigned a name. You could create a style called *title*, for example, that contains all the formatting—font, font size, alignment, and so on—that you normally assign to the titles of your reports. You can use the styles that come with Word or create your own.

Styles help you keep your formatting consistent. They also let you format documents more quickly, because instead of issuing multiple commands to apply formatting codes to a paragraph one by one, you can issue a single command to apply a style that contains all of the codes. Furthermore, if you want to modify the formatting of a document in which you've applied styles, you simply modify the relevant style, and all the text to which you've applied the style is instantly updated.

How to Apply Outline Levels

You apply outline levels to your headings to define a structure of headings and subheadings that Word can use in the Document Map or Outline view. Because outline levels don't affect the appearance of your text, you can think of them as "invisible" formatting. If you want to both define a structure for your document and apply formatting to your headings at the same time, read the remaining three topics in this chapter.

▶ **Instead of choosing Format, Paragraph to display the Paragraph dialog box, you can double-click on the left or right indent marker in the ruler. (See "How to Indent a Paragraph" in Chapter 10 if you need help finding the indent markers.)**

▶ **In addition to letting you use the Document Map and Outline view, outline levels also let you use Word's table of contents feature to automatically generate a table of contents for your document. To find out more about this feature, use the Office Assistant to search the help system for *table of contents* (see Chapter 3).**

1 Click in the paragraph to which you want to apply the outline level.

Waller Street Neighborhood Association

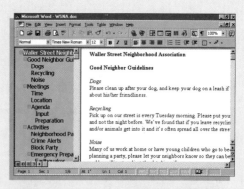

7 Once you have applied outline levels, you will see the hierarchical structure of your document in the Document Map or Outline view (see Chapter 12). In this example, the Document Map shows that four outline levels were applied to the headings in the document.

2 Choose Format, Paragraph to display the Paragraph dialog box.

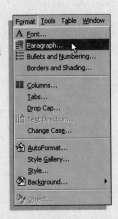

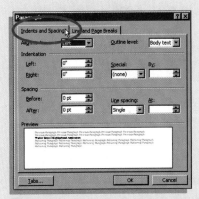

3 Click on the Indents and Spacing tab if it isn't already in front.

Level 1

Level 2

Level 3

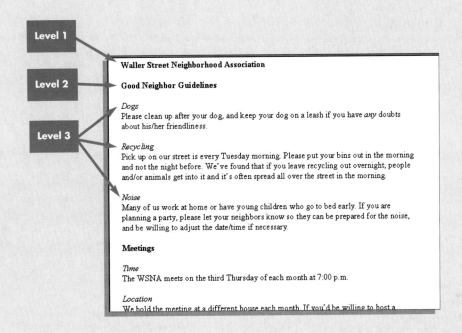

Waller Street Neighborhood Association

Good Neighbor Guidelines

Dogs
Please clean up after your dog, and keep your dog on a leash if you have *any* doubts about his/her friendliness.

Recycling
Pick up on our street is every Tuesday morning. Please put your bins out in the morning and not the night before. We've found that if you leave recycling out overnight, people and/or animals get into it and it's often spread all over the street in the morning.

Noise
Many of us work at home or have young children who go to bed early. If you are planning a party, please let your neighbors know so they can be prepared for the noise, and be willing to adjust the date/time if necessary.

Meetings

Time
The WSNA meets on the third Thursday of each month at 7:00 p.m.

Location
We hold the meeting at a different house each month. If you'd be willing to host a

4 Display the Outline Level drop-down list, and click on the desired level. Use Level 1 for the main headings in your document, Level 2 for subheadings within your main headings, and so on.

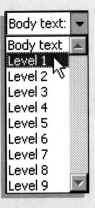

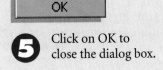

5 Click on OK to close the dialog box.

6 Repeat steps 1 through 5 for each heading in your document.

How to Apply Styles

Word divides styles into two types: character and paragraph. *Character* styles can only contain character formatting, while *paragraph* styles can contain both character and paragraph formatting. Because paragraph styles are more flexible, the examples in this chapter focus on this type. By default, Word automatically creates and applies styles based on your formatting. This can make it difficult to understand how to apply styles yourself, so you might want to temporarily disable this feature until you have a good grasp of how styles work. At that point, you can decide whether to turn the feature back on again.

▶ **1** Choose Tools, AutoCorrect to display the AutoCorrect dialog box.

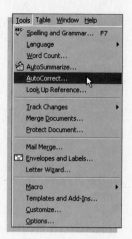

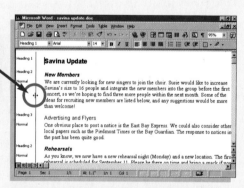

Drag to the left to hide the style area.

8 Word now displays the names of the styles next to the paragraphs to which they are applied. To later hide the style area, simply drag the border to the far left edge of the document window and release the mouse.

2 Click on the AutoFormat As You Type tab, clear the check box labeled "Define Styles Based on Your Formatting," and then click on OK. (To later turn this feature back on, simply repeat these two steps, this time marking the check box.)

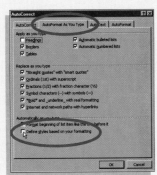

Savina |Update

3 To apply a style, first click in the desired paragraph.

4 Display the Style list in the Formatting toolbar. The styles you see vary depending on what template you are using and on whether you've created styles of your own. Note that Word displays style names in the style's actual font. The gray box to the right of each name shows the style's font size and alignment, and indicates whether the style is a character (a) or paragraph (¶) style. Click on the style you want to apply.

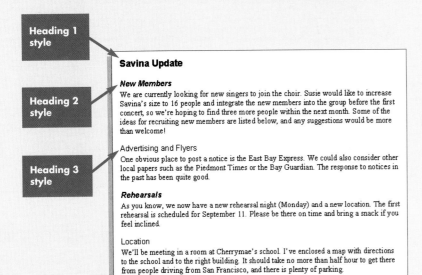

Heading 1 style

Heading 2 style

Heading 3 style

Savina Update

New Members
We are currently looking for new singers to join the choir. Susie would like to increase Savina's size to 16 people and integrate the new members into the group before the first concert, so we're hoping to find three more people within the next month. Some of the ideas for recruiting new members are listed below, and any suggestions would be more than welcome!

Advertising and Flyers
One obvious place to post a notice is the East Bay Express. We could also consider other local papers such as the Piedmont Times or the Bay Guardian. The response to notices in the past has been quite good.

Rehearsals
As you know, we now have a new rehearsal night (Monday) and a new location. The first rehearsal is scheduled for September 11. Please be there on time and bring a snack if you feel inclined.

Location
We'll be meeting in a room at Cherrymae's school. I've enclosed a map with directions to the school and to the right building. It should take no more than half hour to get there from people driving from San Francisco, and there is plenty of parking.

Savina Update

5 The style is applied to the paragraph containing your insertion point. The Heading 1 style applied in this example contains codes for Arial, 14-point, boldface font with some spacing applied before and after the paragraph. (Spacing before and after is a paragraph formatting feature available in the Paragraph dialog box.)

New|Members

7 Another way you can see what styles you've applied in your document is to display their names along the left edge of the document window. Choose Tools, Options, click on the View tab, and change the inch measurement in the Style Area Width box to about 0.6. Then click on OK to close the dialog box. (The Style Area Width option is only available in Normal view.)

6 You can check what style has been applied to a paragraph by clicking in the paragraph and then looking at the Style list. In this example, the insertion point is in the *New Members* heading, and the Style list indicates that the paragraph is formatted with the Heading 2 style. The Formatting toolbar also shows you some of the formatting in the current style. Here, you can see that the Heading 2 style includes an Arial, 12-point, boldface, italic font.

How to Create Styles

You can create your own styles (*user-defined styles*) in a variety of ways. The method shown here uses the Style dialog box. This technique lets you add the style to the template so that it will be available to any document you create that's based on the same template. If you opt not to add a style to the template, the style is only saved with the active document. If you haven't already done so, follow steps 1 and 2 on the previous page to temporarily disable Word's automatic style feature while you practice creating your own styles. You can turn the feature back on at any time.

TIP SHEET

▶ If you consistently use a set of styles in a particular order, you can link them together so that when you press Enter to end a paragraph formatted with one style, Word automatically selects the style for the following paragraph. Using the sample document on this page as an example, you could link the styles so that Bird Name is automatically followed by Description, Description is followed by Price, and Price is followed by Bird Name. In the New Style dialog box, specify a style to follow the one you're creating by choosing it from the Style for Following Paragraph list.

▶ If you want to make use of the Document Map and Outline view, but don't want to modify Word's default heading styles (Heading 1, Heading 2, and so on), create your own heading styles with different names, but include the appropriate outline level in each style. (In step 5, choose Paragraph from the Format button and select the desired level from the Outline Level list.)

1 Choose Format, Style to display the Style dialog box. (It doesn't matter where your insertion point is located when you issue this command.)

8 The new style is added to the Style list box in the Formatting toolbar. Here, the style list contains the new style Bird Name, as well as two other user-defined styles, Description and Price.

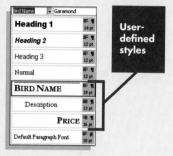

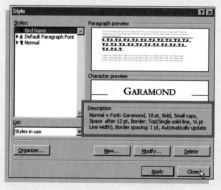

7 Repeat steps 5 and 6 as necessary to add all desired formatting to the new style, and then click on OK to return to the Style dialog box. In this example, paragraph and border formatting codes were added to the Bird Name style to add spacing after the paragraph and a top border. The Description area lists the formatting codes you've added to the style. Click on Close to close the Style dialog box. (Only click on the Apply button if you want to apply the new style to whatever paragraph your insertion point is resting in at the moment.)

2 Click on the New button to display the New Style dialog box.

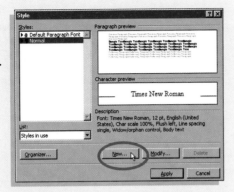

3 Type a name for the new style in the Name text box. Spaces are allowed in style names. Check to make sure that Paragraph is listed under Style Type, and that Normal is displayed under Based On.

Bird Name style   **Description style**   **Price style**

LawnBirds' Spring Selection

FLAMINGO

The flamingo is our premier lawn bird. Tall, elegant, graceful, yet whimsical too. With its colorful plumage, the flamingo has added charm to lawns and gardens for many years.

PRICE: 23.00

GREAT EGRET

One of the newest additions to our line, the egret is the most regal of our birds. Its long silky white plumage and stately air will bring a still calm to your garden that many people find reminiscent of the misty marshes where egrets live in the wild.

PRICE: 35.50

ROSEATE SPOONBILL

With its long spatulate bill, pale pink body, and unfeathered greenish head, the spoonbill is a truly distinctive lawn bird. If you've ever wished for a conversation starter, this is the bird for you.

4 If you want to save this style with the template, mark the Add to Template check box. Optionally mark the Automatically Update check box. If this feature is enabled, then when you later modify the formatting of a paragraph to which you've applied the style, Word updates the style itself to match the new formatting of the paragraph. As a result, any other paragraphs to which you've applied the same style are also updated to match the appearance of the paragraph you modified.

6 Select the settings you want included in the style, then click on OK to return to the New Style dialog box. Here, the formatting codes for a Garamond, boldface, 18-point font in small caps will be added to the Bird Name style.

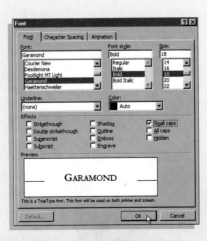

5 Click on the Format button. The options in the Format list—Font, Paragraph, Tabs, Border, and so on—lead to the dialog boxes you normally use to apply character and paragraph formatting. Click an option that leads to a dialog box containing formatting features you want to include in the style.

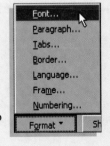

How to Modify Styles

By making a quick modification to a style, you can reformat a certain text element throughout your entire document. For example, if you've used a style called *sectionhead* for 20 headings in a long report, and later decide the headings should be in a larger font, you only need to modify the sectionhead style, and all 20 headings will be reformatted instantly. The steps for modifying a style are very similar to those for creating a new style described on the previous page.

1 Choose Format, Style to display the Style dialog box.

TIP SHEET

▸ **If you have marked the Update Automatically check box for a style (available in the New Style and Modify Style dialog boxes), you can modify a style simply by revising the formatting in a paragraph to which the style is applied. However, when you modify a style in this way, the modified version is saved in the document only, not in the template. If you want to save the modified version in the template, follow the steps on this page, being sure to mark the Add to Template check box in step 3.**

▸ **To delete a style, choose Format, Style to display the Style dialog box. On the left side of the dialog box, click on the style to be deleted, then click on the Delete button. Click on Yes when Word confirms you want to delete the style.**

▸ **By default, the Styles dialog box lists the styles that are in use in the current document. In step 2, if you want to modify a style that isn't used in the current document, display the drop-down list under List in the lower-left corner of the dialog box, and choose All styles.**

7 All the paragraphs to which you've applied the style are now reformatted with the modified version (see the sample document in the middle of the page).

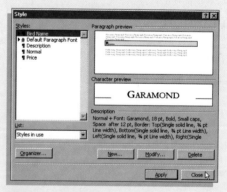

6 Repeat steps 4 and 5 to make additional modifications to the style if necessary. When you're finished, click on OK, and click on Close to close the Style dialog box. (Only click on the Apply button if you want to apply the modified style to whatever paragraph your insertion point is resting in at the moment.)

2 In the list of styles on the left side of the dialog box, click on the style you want to modify (Bird Name in this example). Then click on the Modify button to display the Modify Style dialog box. With the exception of the name in the title bar, this dialog box is identical to the New Style dialog box shown on the previous page. (If you don't see the style you want to modify in the Styles list, see the Tip Sheet.)

3 If you want to modify the style for the active document only, leave the Add to Template check box cleared. If, however, you want to use the modified version of the style in all future documents you create based on the template, mark the check box. (The modified version of the style does not replace the original version in documents you've already created.)

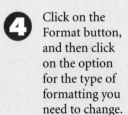

4 Click on the Format button, and then click on the option for the type of formatting you need to change.

The Bird Name style has been modified.

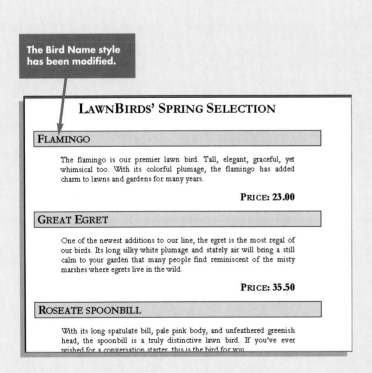

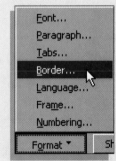

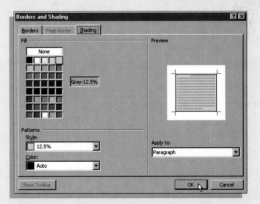

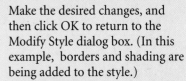

5 Make the desired changes, and then click OK to return to the Modify Style dialog box. (In this example, borders and shading are being added to the style.)

CHAPTER 14

Templates

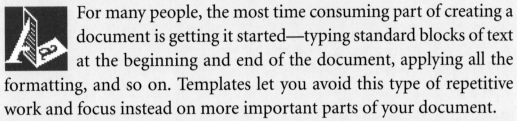For many people, the most time consuming part of creating a document is getting it started—typing standard blocks of text at the beginning and end of the document, applying all the formatting, and so on. Templates let you avoid this type of repetitive work and focus instead on more important parts of your document.

As mentioned in earlier chapters, a *template* is a rough blueprint for a document that usually includes some combination of text and formatting. When you start a new document, Word assumes you want to base it on the Normal template unless you specify otherwise. The Normal template (also called the *Blank Document template*) starts you off with a "plain vanilla" document. It doesn't include any text, and it includes only the most basic formatting: single line spacing, left alignment, Times New Roman 10-point font, and so forth.

In addition to the Normal template, Word ships with almost 40 other templates for creating memos, letters, fax cover sheets, reports, calendars, and even Web pages. In this chapter, you learn how to use these other templates, and you find out how to create and modify your own.

How to Use a Template

Word's templates are well-designed and easy to use. A "paint-by-numbers" approach to document creation, templates show you exactly what type of text to enter where. In fact, you may notice fancy formatting in some templates that you don't quite understand and wouldn't know how to create yourself. Don't worry about it. The beauty of using a template is that you can let Word handle the formatting for you.

TIP SHEET

▶ **The advantage of using a template instead of an ordinary document to store text and formatting you want to reuse is that you can't accidentally overwrite a template. When you start a document based on a template, "fill in the blanks," and save, Word saves the document separately from the template, leaving the template in its original form. In contrast, if you open a document you're using as a "blueprint," revise it, and then accidentally use File, Save instead of File, Save As to save the "filled-in" version, you overwrite the original document and lose your blueprint.**

▶ **Some templates, such as the one on this page, include a sentence or two of instructions in the body of the document. Once you've read the instructions, simply select the text and type over it.**

▶ **Be sure to check the header and footer areas of the template. Many templates have "dummy text" in these areas that needs to be replaced. See Chapter 12 if you need help working with headers and footers.**

▶ **If necessary, you can attach a template to an existing document. Choose Tools, Templates and Add-Ins and click on the Attach button. Select the desired template (it will be stored in the Templates folder or in one of its subfolders), and click on OK. If you want the styles in the document to be updated to match the styles in the template you just attached, mark the Automatically Update Document Styles check box, and then click on OK.**

 1 Choose File, New to display the New dialog box. In this situation, you can't use the New button on the Standard toolbar as a shortcut. (When you click on the New button, Word assumes you want to start a new document based on the Normal template; it doesn't give you the chance to choose a different template.)

8 When you have completed the document, use the regular methods to save, print, and close it.

7 The text you typed replaces the "click here" text. Continue in the same fashion, replacing all the "click here" instructions with the text you want in the document.

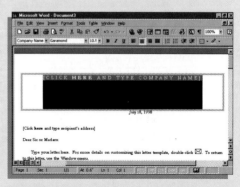

 6 Click on the first "click here" instruction to select it, and type your text.

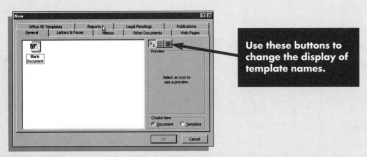

Use these buttons to change the display of template names.

2 The Normal (Blank Document) template is stored in the General tab. Click on the other tabs at the top of the dialog box to see what additional templates are available. Depending on how Word was installed and whether anyone has created new templates, the tabs and templates you see may differ from those shown here. You can change the display of the template names by clicking on the Large Icon, List, and Detail buttons.

3 Try clicking on a few template names. When a template is selected, Word displays a preview of it on the right side of the dialog box (if a preview is available). Here, the Contemporary Report template in the Reports tab is selected.

Template   **Completed document**

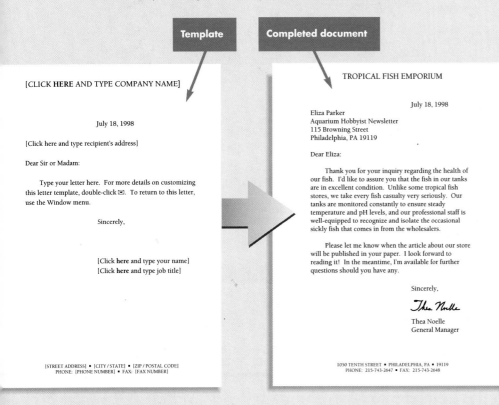

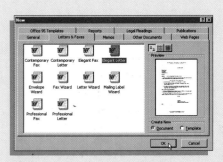

4 Some templates are called Wizards. *Wizards* are specialized templates that let you customize the document you create (see the next page). The Letters & Faxes tab shown here contains Wizards for creating envelopes, faxes, letters, and mailing labels. When you find the template you want to use (Elegant Letter in this example), click on it, and then click on the OK button.

5 Word creates a new document based on the template you chose. Many templates, including the one shown here, provide instructions to "Click here and type" to help you fill in your text. You may also see some cross-hatched boxes. Word uses these for formatting purposes only—they won't print out.

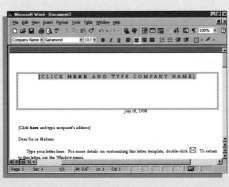

How to Use a Wizard

Wizards differ from standard templates in two ways: They offer a great deal of hand-holding, and they let you tailor the template to suit your preferences. Wizards typically ask you a series of questions about what text and formatting you want included in the document. When a Wizard has gathered all the information it needs, it presents you with a document that conforms to your requests. Wizard-generated documents look just like documents based on standard templates (see the preceding page), complete with "click here" instructions to help you fill in the text.

TIP SHEET

▶ **If you've used a Wizard before and know that you want to keep all the default answers to the questions, you can click the Finish button on the Start page (see step 3) to complete the "questionnaire" without changing the default choices.**

▶ **Some Wizards display the document at a reduced zoom setting so that you can see more of it on your screen. If you want to enlarge the document to make it easier to read, display the Zoom Control list in the Standard toolbar, and click on 100%. You may then need to use the horizontal scroll bar to scroll the right and left margins into view (see "How to Zoom In and Out" in Chapter 4).**

 1 Choose File, New to display the New dialog box. Remember, you cannot use the New button on the Standard toolbar as a shortcut in this situation.

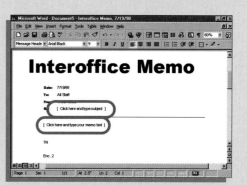

6 After a moment or two, Word displays a document in Page Layout view with the text and formatting you requested. Wherever you see "click here" instructions, replace them with actual text. Then save, print, and close the document.

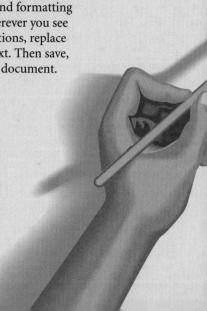

2 Click on the tab that contains the Wizard you want to use, click on the Wizard name, and click on OK to start it. (This example uses the Memo Wizard in the Memos tab.)

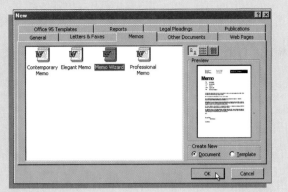

Interoffice Memo

Date: 7/19/98

To: All Staff

From: Thea Noelle

RE: Floaters

It has come to my attention that there have been a large number of floaters observed by customers in the tanks in recent weeks. This scares away customers and creates a horrible image for the store. Please do your utmost to a) keep them from dying in the first place, b) if they do die, remove them immediately!

For newer staff members, I'm enclosing two handouts that will help you spot the signs of a fish that isn't long for this world. Read them!

Your attention to this matter would be most appreciated. A bonus will be handed out at the end of the month to the staff of the area with the lowest number of reported floaters.

TN

Enc. 2

3 Word displays the first "page" of the Wizard dialog box, called *Start*. As you progress through the Wizard, Word highlights the current step on the left side of the dialog box. Click on the Next button to move to the next step.

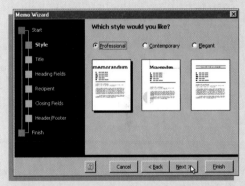

4 The Wizard presents the first question. In this example, it needs to know which style you prefer for your memo. Make your selection, and click on Next again. Continue working your way through the steps. If you want to go back to a previous step, click the Back button one or more times.

5 When you reach the Finish step, click on the Finish button to tell the Wizard to start generating the document.

How to Create Your Own Template

The templates that come with Word are attractive and carefully crafted. But if you want to use templates for form letters or other types of customized documents, you will need to create your own. When you create a template "from scratch," you can add to it the exact text and formatting you need.

▶ If you like one of the existing templates, you may want to use it as a basis for creating your own template. That way, you can keep its general layout and tweak it to suit your needs. Instead of clicking on the Blank Document template in step 2, click on the template you want to use. Then in step 4, fill in all the "click here" text you want to personalize, and make any other modifications to the text or formatting.

▶ Notice that in step 8, a preview of the TFE Letterhead template is showing. Follow these instructions if you want Word to display a preview of the templates you create in the New dialog box: In step 4, choose File, Properties, mark the Save Preview Picture check box in the lower-left corner of the Properties dialog box, and click on OK.

▶ **1** Choose File, New to display the New dialog box.

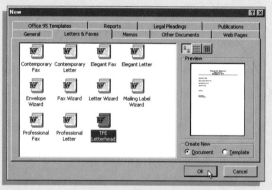

8 When you want to use your new template, choose File, New, click on the appropriate tab in the New dialog box, click on the template name, and click on OK.

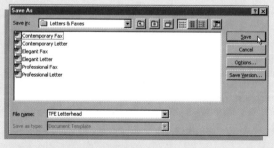

7 Type a name for the template, click on the Save button, and then close the template.

2 Click on the General tab if it's not already active, and then click on the Blank Document template.

3 Click on the Template option button under Create New in the lower-right corner of the dialog box. This tells Word that you want to create an actual template, not a document based on the selected template. Then click on OK.

Tropical Fish Emporium
1050 Tenth Street
Philadelphia, PA 19119

September 18, 1998

[Type recipient's address here]

Dear [Type name here]:

[Type letter here]

Sincerely,

Thea Noelle
General Manager

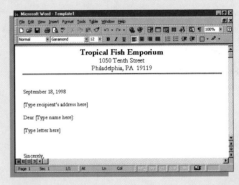

4 Word creates a blank template for you. Observe that the name in the title bar is *Template1*, instead of the usual *Document1*. Enter all the text and formatting you want. If you like, you can put in "dummy text" where the user needs to fill in information. (The user will need to select these instructions and type over them.) You may also want to insert the date as a field so that it will be updated each time you use the template (see Chapter 8).

5 Choose File, Save As to display the Save As dialog box.

6 Word stores all its templates in the Templates folder (which is normally a subfolder of Microsoft Office) or in a subfolder under Templates. If you save your new template in the Templates folder itself, the template will appear in the General tab of the New dialog box. If you save it in one of the subfolders, it will appear in the corresponding tab in the New dialog box. In this example, the template is being saved in the Letters & Faxes subfolder, so it will show up in the Letters & Faxes tab of the New dialog box.

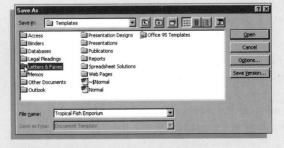

How to Modify a Template

After using a template for a while, you may notice some text or formatting you want to change. While you can make the change in each document you base on that template, it's much more efficient to modify the template itself. Remember that merely modifying a document based on the template does not in any way affect the underlying template. You need to open the template itself and revise it, as described on this page.

1 Click on the Open button in the Standard toolbar (or choose File, Open).

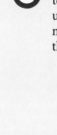

6 Save and close the template. When you use the template the next time, you'll see the modified version.

TIP SHEET

▸ Remember, you do not follow the steps described on this page if you simply want to use the template to create a document. If you do so accidentally, you'll end up overwriting the blank template with the filled-in version. Instead, follow the steps in "How to Use a Template" earlier in this chapter.

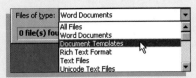

2 In the Open dialog box, choose Document Templates from the Files of Type list (located in the lower-left corner of the dialog box).

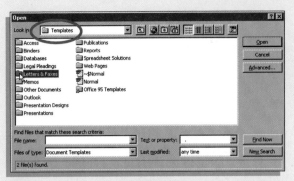

3 Double-click on the folder in which the template is stored—either the Templates folder itself or a subfolder of Templates. (The Templates folder is usually a subfolder of the Microsoft Office folder. If you can't find it, ask your resident computer guru for help.)

Revised letterhead

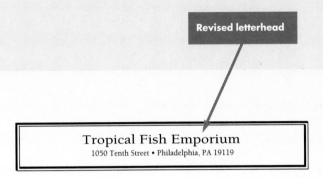

Tropical Fish Emporium
1050 Tenth Street • Philadelphia, PA 19119

September 18, 1998

[Type recipient's address here]

Dear [Type name here]:

[Type letter here]

Sincerely,

Thea Noelle
General Manager

Owned and Operated By Genuine Fish Fanatics

New footer

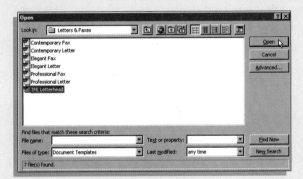

4 Click on the template (TFE Letterhead in this example), and then click on the Open button.

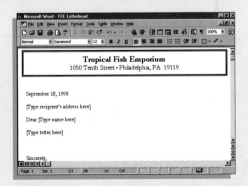

5 Make your changes to the text or formatting of the template. In this example, a box border is added to the letterhead, the address is reformatted to fit on one line, and a footer is added.

CHAPTER 15

Columns and Tables

 Word's columns feature creates *newspaper-style* columns—that is, columns in which the text flows down one column, then snakes up to the top of the next. You might want to use columns in newsletters, bulletins, journal articles, and so on. In this chapter, you learn how to create columns, how to apply columns to only part of a document, and how to modify column formatting.

If you need to create a simple columnar list in which the text *does not* snake from one column to the next, you can use custom tabs (see Chapter 10). If you want to create a more complex list or chart, the best option is to use a Word table. A *table* is a grid of rows and columns, and each "box" in a table is called a *cell*.

Tables are incredibly flexible; you can use them to create anything from simple charts to invoices, employee lists, or resumes. Once you've inserted a table in your document, you can change its structure by adding or deleting rows or columns, changing column widths, and so on. You can also format tables in many different ways, choosing what type of borders you want (if any), whether to add shading to any of the cells, how to align the text within each cell, and so on.

You can enter numbers into a table and perform simple calculations on them, but if you need to work extensively with numerical data, you'll probably want to use a spreadsheet program such as Excel instead. The table feature's strong suit is handling text, and in this respect it is much more powerful than spreadsheet programs.

How to Create Columns

You can create columns using either the Columns dialog box (Format, Columns) or the Columns button on the Standard toolbar. The toolbar button is the faster method, although the dialog box comes in handy when you want to change the formatting of columns (see the next page). You can edit a document after you've applied columns, but it's usually easier to type and edit your text first, and then apply columns as a last step before printing. As with other page-formatting features, columns automatically affect the entire document unless you divide the document into sections. If you don't want columns in part of your document, follow steps 1 through 4 to insert a section break. Otherwise, begin with step 5.

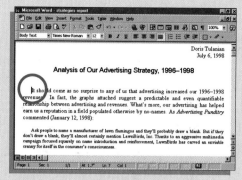

► **1** Position your insertion point at the location where you want the columns to begin.

8 To change the number of columns, simply repeat steps 6 and 7, this time pointing to a different number of columns.

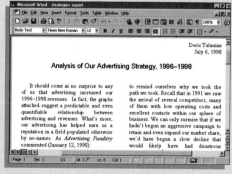

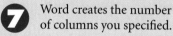

7 Word creates the number of columns you specified.

2 Choose Insert, Break to display the Break dialog box.

3 If you want the columns to begin at the top of the next page, click the Next Page option button to insert a *next page* section break. If you want the columns to stay on the same page as the text above the section break, click the Continuous option button to insert a *continuous* section break. Then click on OK, and make sure to keep the insertion point in the section to which you want to apply the columns.

It should come as no surprise to any of us that advertising inc revenues. In fact, the graphs attached suggest a predictable

4 Word places a section break in your document. In this example, a continuous section break allows the document title (in section 1) and the document text (in section 2) to stay on the same page.

LawnBirds, Inc.

Doris Tulanian
July 6, 1998

Analysis of Our Advertising Strategy, 1996-1998

It should come as no surprise to any of us that advertising increased our 1996-1998 revenues. In fact, the graphs attached suggest a predictable and even quantifiable relationship. What's more, our advertising has helped earn us a reputation in a field populated otherwise by no-names. As *Advertising Punditry* commented (January 12, 1998):

Ask people to name a manufacturer of lawn flamingos and they'll probably draw a blank. But if they don't draw a blank, they'll almost certainly mention LawnBirds, Inc. Thanks to an aggressive multimedia campaign focused squarely on name introduction and reinforcement, LawnBirds has carved an enviable cranny for itself in the consumer's consciousness.

The question, then, is not whether advertising sells lawn flamingos. It does. The question is how many lawn flamingos advertising sells. Do the increased revenues make up our costs? If they have so far, will they continue to? Do the economics call for increasing our ad budget, stabilizing it, decreasing it, or shifting it among the different media?

This analysis attempts to point our advertising in the right direction for the immediate future. However, we must note one obvious constraint: Any hindsight as to what our revenues and profits would have been without advertising is little

more than guesswork. The most we can do is project our growth from our preadvertising years and factor in those marketplace changes that we understand and that are quantifiable.

Why did we start advertising in the first place? It's worthwhile occasionally to remind ourselves why we took the path we took. Recall that in 1991 we saw the arrival of several competitors, many of them with low operating costs and excellent contacts within our sphere of business. We can only surmise that if we hadn't begun an aggressive campaign to retain and even expand our market share, we'd have begun a slow decline that would likely have had disastrous consequences for our company.

Fortunately, we had a team of farsighted individuals who read the writing on the wall, and began planning an in-depth strategy that has, we are pleased to report, proved enormously successful. They began by surveying our customers to find out just what the lawn bird (particularly the lawn flamingo) represents to the average American home owner.

The results they came up with were predictable. In the minds of our customers, the lawn bird seems to represent a sense of security, stability, and neighborliness. People feel their birds reflect their commitment to keeping up the appearance of their yards and help to create a friendly and inviting

5 Choose View, Page Layout to switch to Page Layout view. Word can't display columns in Normal view, so it's easiest if you switch to Page Layout view before creating them.

6 Click on the Columns button on the Standard toolbar. A grid drops down containing vertical bars representing columns. Point to the number of columns you want, and click once.

How to Format Columns

You can, of course, apply all the usual character, paragraph, and page formatting to multiple-column text as you would to ordinary text. For example, in the sample document shown here, the first line of each paragraph is indented one quarter inch, the document text is justified, and the quotation in the left column was formatted in a smaller font size. Here you'll find a few suggestions for some additional formatting options that can enhance the appearance of your columns.

▶ **The last page of a multiple-column document can look awkward if there is not enough text to fill all the columns. To balance the columns on the last page so that they're approximately the same length, follow these steps to insert a continuous section break at the end of the last column:**

▶ **Press Ctrl+End to move the insertion point to the end of the document**

▶ **Choose Insert, Break**

▶ **Click on the Continuous option button**

▶ **Click on OK**

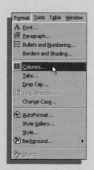

1 Click in the multiple-column text, and then choose Format, Columns to display the Columns dialog box.

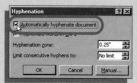

7 In the Hyphenation dialog box, mark the Automatically Hyphenate Document check box, and click on OK.

6 With columns of justified text, you can reduce the obvious gaps between words by turning on hyphenation (see document in the middle of this page). To do this, first choose Tools, Language, Hyphenation.

2 The top of the dialog box contains some pre-set formats for multiple columns of varying numbers and widths. Click on one of them to make your columns match that format. You can also change the number of columns by entering a number in the Number of Columns text box. You can preview your changes in the lower-right corner of the dialog box.

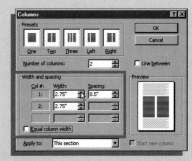

3 If you have specific requirements for the width of each column and the amount of space between columns, clear the Equal Column Width check box, and then enter the desired settings for each column under Width and Spacing.

LawnBirds, Inc.

Doris Tulanian
July 6, 1998

Analysis of Our Advertising Strategy, 1996-1998

It should come as no surprise to any of us that advertising increased our 1996-1998 revenues. In fact, the graphs attached suggest a predict-able and even quantifiable relation-ship. What's more, our advertising has helped earn us a reputation in a field populated otherwise by no-names. As *Advertising Punditry* commented (January 12, 1998):

Ask people to name a manufactur-er of lawn flamingos and they'll prob-ably draw a blank. But if they don't draw a blank, they'll almost certainly mention LawnBirds, Inc. Thanks to an aggressive multimedia campaign fo-cused squarely on name introduction and reinforcement, LawnBirds has carved an enviable cranny for itself in the consumer's consciousness.

The question, then, is not wheth-er advertising sells lawn flamingos. It does. The question is how many lawn flamingos advertising sells. Do the increased revenues make up our costs? If they have so far, will they continue to? Do the economics call for increasing our ad budget, stabiliz-ing it, decreasing it, or shifting it among the different media?

This analysis attempts to point our advertising in the right direction for the immediate future. However, we must note one obvious con-straint: Any hindsight as to what our revenues and profits would have been without advertising is little more than guesswork. The most we

can do is project our growth from our preadvertising years and factor in those marketplace changes that we understand and that are quantifiable.

Why did we start advertising in the first place? It's worthwhile occa-sionally to remind ourselves why we took the path we took. Recall that in 1991 we saw the arrival of several competitors, many of them with low operating costs and excellent con-tacts within our sphere of business. We can only surmise that if we hadn't begun an aggressive cam-paign to retain and even expand our market share, we'd have begun a slow decline that would likely have had disastrous consequences for our company.

Fortunately, we had a team of farsighted individuals who read the writing on the wall, and began plan-ning an in-depth strategy that has, we are pleased to report, proved enor-mously successful. They began by surveying our customers to find out just what the lawn bird (particularly the lawn flamingo) represents to the average American home owner.

The results they came up with were predictable. In the minds of our customers, the lawn bird seems to represent a sense of security, stabili-ty, and neighborliness. People feel their birds reflect their commitment to keeping up the appearance of their yards and help to create a friendly and inviting atmosphere in their community.

Taking the responses to the mar-

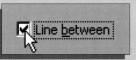

4 To add vertical lines between your columns, mark the Line Between check box.

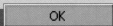

5 Click on OK when you've made your selections.

How to Create a Table

Word lets you create tables in two ways: You can use the Table, Insert Table command (or the Insert Table button on the Standard toolbar) to specify how many rows and columns you want, and Word then creates the empty table for you. Alternatively, you can use the Draw Table button on the Tables and Borders toolbar to draw the table with your mouse. This method is the most flexible, so it's the one you'll learn here. Regardless of how you insert the table, you can easily adjust the number of rows and columns at any time (see the next page).

TIP SHEET

▶ **If you want to create a large table, it's faster to use the Insert Table command than to draw the table with the mouse. Choose Table, Insert Table, type the number of rows and columns you want in the Insert Table dialog box, and click on OK. (You can also click on the Insert Table button in the Standard toolbar and drag across the desired number of rows and columns in the grid that drops down.)**

▶ **To insert a tab in a cell, press Ctrl+Tab; pressing the Tab key by itself moves the insertion point from cell to cell.**

▶ **If you inserted a table at the very top of a document and later decide you want to type text above the table, click at the very beginning of the upper-left cell in the table and press Enter. Word inserts a blank line above the table and places your insertion point in it so you can start typing.**

▶ **1** Choose View, Page Layout to switch to Page Layout view.

Pressing Enter here forced text down to the next line.

California and
New York

8 The Enter key functions the same way in a table as it does in ordinary text—each time you press it, you insert a paragraph mark, forcing any text to the right of the insertion point down to the next line. If you want to see where you've pressed Enter in a table, click on the Show/Hide button in the Standard toolbar. As with normal text, you use Backspace or Delete to remove paragraph marks.

	Flamingo	Great Egret	Roseate Spoonbill
Selling Points	Looks good in small flocks	Especially attractive with vines trailing up its legs	Maintains color very well
Flaws	Frequently develops cracks in its tail	Has been known to scare dogs and small children	Tends to lean to one side in windy areas
Best-Selling Regions	Florida and the Northwest	New England and the Midwest	California and New York

7 Enter text into the cells. If the entry in a cell is too wide to fit, Word automatically wraps the text to the next line and increases the row height to accommodate the text.

2 Click on the Tables and Borders button on the Standard toolbar.

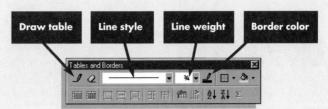

Draw table   Line style   Line weight   Border color

3 Word displays the Tables and Borders toolbar floating over the document window. (See "How to Customize the Toolbars" in Chapter 4 if you need help positioning the toolbar.) Click on the Draw Table button if it isn't already selected, then use the Line Style, Line Weight, and Border Color lists to choose the type of line you want to use for the outside border of your table.

Word's Draw Table button makes it easy to create complex tables.

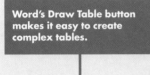

COLOR AVAILABILITY
NOVEMBER 1998

Lawn Bird	Flamingo			Great Egret			Roseate Spoonbill		
Size	S	M	L	S	M	L	S	M	L
Aqua	✓	✓	✓	✓		✓	✓	✓	✓
Fuchsia		✓			✓	✓	✓	✓	
Rose	✓	✓		✓	✓	✓		✓	✓
Sienna		✓	✓	✓		✓	✓	✓	✓

(Color)

Release the mouse when the table is the desired size.

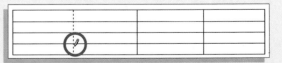

Date: March 15, 1998
To: All sales reps
From: Marketing
Subject: Update

The following table summarizes the most up-to-date information about our top-selling lawn birds. We hope you find it useful.

4 Move the mouse into the document window, and notice that when the Draw Table button is selected, the mouse pointer becomes a small pencil. Starting at the upper-left corner of where you want the table to go, drag diagonally down and to the right, releasing the mouse when the outline of the table is approximately the right size.

6 You can navigate in a table by clicking in the desired cell with your mouse. You can also use the four arrow keys, although if a cell contains text, the right and left arrow keys move the insertion point character by character within the cell. Lastly, you can press Tab to move cell by cell to the right, and Shift+Tab to move to the left. When a cell contains text, pressing Tab or Shift+Tab selects the contents of the cell you move into.

5 Select a different type of line if desired (see step 3), and draw the lines for the rows and columns. As you drag, a dashed line shows you where the line will be inserted. Release the mouse as the line extends across the entire width or height of the table. You can draw a simple table such as the one shown here, or a complex one such as the one in the middle of the page.

How to Change the Structure of a Table

As you enter text into a table, you will almost certainly need to make some structural changes. This page describes the most common adjustments you'll need to make. As you experiment with these techniques, keep in mind that Word does not prevent you from making a table too wide to fit on the page. If you're adding columns and changing column widths, check Print Preview periodically to make sure the table isn't running off the page.

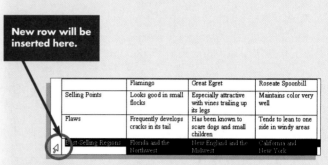

New row will be inserted here.

1 To insert a new row in the middle of the table, begin by selecting the row below the location of the new one. Select the row by clicking to the left of it, with the mouse pointer outside of the table. (Make sure the Draw Table button in the Tables and Borders toolbar is turned off.)

8 In the Cell Height and Width dialog box, click on the Row tab if it isn't already active, click on the desired alignment option, and click on OK.

7 By default, tables are aligned along the left margin of the page. If you want to change the alignment, begin by choosing Table, Cell Height and Width.

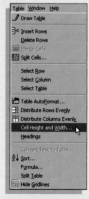

2 Once the row is selected, click on the Insert Rows button on the Standard toolbar. (When a row is selected, this button replaces the Insert Table button.) If you want to insert a row at the bottom of the table, just click in the last cell of the table (the lower-right cell) and press the Tab key.

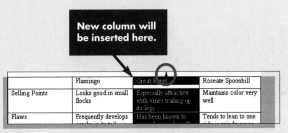

3 To add a new column, first select the column to the right of where the new one will go. (Again, make sure the Draw Table button is turned off.) Point to the top boundary of the column. When the mouse pointer changes to a small black arrow, click once. If you want to add a column at the right end of the table, select the column of *end-of-row markers* just outside the right edge of the table. (You can display these markers by clicking on the Show/Hide button in the Standard toolbar.)

	Flamingo	Great Egret	Roseate Spoonbill
Selling Points	Looks good in small flocks	Especially attractive with vines trailing up its legs	Maintains color very well
Flaws	Frequently develops cracks in its tail	Has been known to scare dogs and small children	Tends to lean to one side in windy areas
Best-Selling Regions	Florida and the Northwest		

Joe, the table looks great, but could you add a column for the White-Faced Ibis?

Thanks, Tina

4 Once the column is selected, click on the Insert Columns button in the Standard toolbar. (When a column is selected, this button replaces the Insert Table button.)

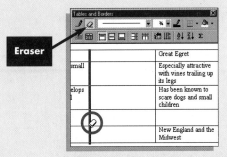

5 To delete a line in a table, click on the Eraser button in the Tables and Borders toolbar (the mouse pointer becomes an eraser), then drag over the line you want to delete. As soon as the line is selected, release the mouse. When you erase the line between two cells, you actually merge the cells into one large cell. If you want to keep the cells separate but just remove the border between them, see the Tip Sheet on the next page.

	Flamingo
Selling Points	Looks good in small flocks
Flaws	Frequently develops cracks in its tail
Best-Selling Regions	Florida and the Northwest

6 To adjust the width of a column, point to the right column boundary so the mouse pointer becomes a double black arrow, and then drag the column boundary to the left (to narrow the column) or to the right (to widen the column). You can also adjust the height of a row by dragging the row boundary up or down.

How to Format a Table

Formatting a table involves changing both the appearance of the text (by applying character and paragraph formatting) and the appearance of the cells themselves (by adding borders and shading). Be careful to select the exact cells you want to format before using the commands described on this page, and remember that you can always use Undo if you make a change you don't like.

TIP SHEET

▶ If you want to remove a border, click on the Border button in the Tables and Borders toolbar, choose the No Border option, then click on the Draw Table button and drag over the borders you want to remove.

▶ To remove shading, first click in the cell whose shading you want to remove. Or, if you want to remove shading from several cells, make sure the Draw Table button is turned off, and then drag across the cells to select them. Next, click on the Shading Color button in the Tables and Borders toolbar, and click on the None option at the top of the color palette.

▶ You can rotate text in a cell so that it displays vertically. Click in the cell that contains the text, and click one or more times on the Change Text Direction button in the Tables and Borders toolbar. (For an example, refer to the central graphic image in "How to Create a Table" earlier in this chapter. The word *color* at the left edge of the table is aligned vertically.)

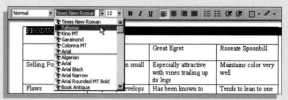

▶ **1** To change the font and font size of text in a table, start by selecting the text. (You can select some of the text within a cell, an entire cell, or a group of cells.) Then use the Formatting toolbar or the Font dialog box (Format, Font) to make the desired changes. In this example, the Tahoma font is being applied to the first row of the table.

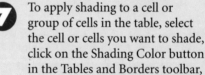

7 To apply shading to a cell or group of cells in the table, select the cell or cells you want to shade, click on the Shading Color button in the Tables and Borders toolbar, and choose the desired color from the palette that drops down. Here, yellow shading is being applied to the top row of the table.

2 To apply boldface, italics, or underline, select the portion of the table you want to affect, then click the appropriate button in the Formatting toolbar. Here, boldface is being applied to the second row of the table.

3 To align text horizontally within each cell, select the cells you want to affect, then click on the desired alignment button in the Formatting toolbar. Here, the lines separating cells in the top row were deleted with the Eraser button (see the previous page), merging the original four cells into one large cell. The Center button will thus align the text *Product Update* in the center of the row.

PRODUCT UPDATE			
	Flamingo	**Great Egret**	**Roseate Spoonbill**
Selling Points	Looks good in small flocks	Especially attractive with vines trailing up its legs	Maintains color very well
Flaws	Frequently develops cracks in its tail	Has been known to scare dogs and small children	Tends to lean to one side in windy areas
Best-Selling Regions	Florida and the Northwest	New England and the Midwest	California and New York

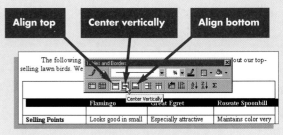

4 Three buttons on the Tables and Borders toolbar—Align Top (the default option), Center Vertically, and Align Bottom—allow you to change the vertical alignment of text. Here, the text in the second row will be centered vertically in the middle of each cell.

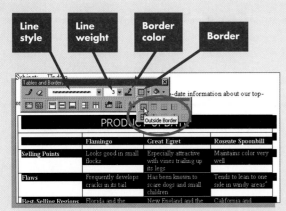

6 Next, select the desired line style, line weight, and border color in the Tables and Borders toolbar, then click on the Border button and choose the Outside Border option. To change individual borders inside the table, select the desired line options, then click on the Draw Table button and draw across the line you want to change. When the line turns gray, release the mouse to apply the new border formatting.

5 To change the border around the outside of the table, first select the entire table by choosing Table, Select Table.

CHAPTER 16

Envelopes and Labels

 Word has streamlined the process of printing envelopes and labels to such an extent that it is largely self-explanatory. Word knows how to format envelopes and labels of various sizes, and if you have typed a letter that is still on your screen, Word can pick out the recipient's address from the top of the letter to use in the envelope or label.

The first two topics in this chapter explain how to prepare and print a standard business envelope, and how to specify a different envelope size if necessary. The last two topics describe how to prepare and print labels, and how to choose a different label size. Word lets you either print a single label or a full page with the same address on each label. As long as you tell Word the product number of the labels, it can position the addresses correctly on each label with no further assistance from you.

How to Prepare and Print an Envelope

To prepare an envelope, you first verify that Word is displaying the correct recipient address and return address, and then you feed the envelope into your printer and issue the command to print. By default, Word formats your envelopes for the United States standard letter size, 4.125 by 9.5 inches, unless you or another user has already reset the envelope size. If you need to change the size, see the next page.

▶ **If you change the return address (step 6), Word asks whether you want to save the new address as the default return address. Click on Yes or No as desired. If you click on Yes, Word enters the new address in the User Information tab of the Options dialog box. You can also change the default return address when you're not in the midst of printing an envelope. To do so, choose Tools, Options, and then click on the User Information tab. Enter the desired information under Name, Initials, and Mailing Address, and click on OK.**

▶ **You can follow the steps on this page regardless of whether a document containing the recipient's address is on screen. You just have to take the extra step of typing the delivery address in step 4.**

▶ **If you have set up a personal address book in Microsoft Outlook (the information management program that ships with MSOffice), you can click on the Insert Address button above the Delivery Address and Return Address boxes to select an address from your personal address book.**

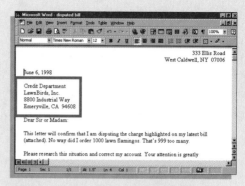

1 If it is convenient, open the letter addressed to the recipient. This will make it slightly faster to prepare the envelope. You don't need to select the recipient's address—Word will find it automatically.

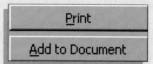

8 Click on the Print button to print the envelope. Or, if you prefer, you can click on the Add to Document button to add the envelope to your document. Word inserts it at the top of the document, separated from the rest of the document by a next page section break. Make sure you have the envelope loaded in the printer before you issue the Print command, because it will print as the first page of your document.

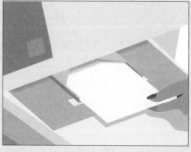

7 Load an envelope into your printer. The Feed box in the Envelopes and Labels dialog box shows you how Word expects you to feed the envelope.

2 Choose Tools, Envelopes and Labels.

3 In the Envelopes and Labels dialog box, click on the Envelopes tab if it is not already active.

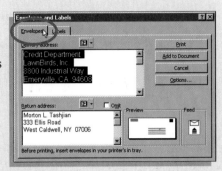

4 Observe the Delivery Address box. Word looks for this address in the active document. If the box is blank or if the address is incorrect, type or edit the address as needed.

5 If you don't want to print a return address on the envelope—most likely because your envelopes have a preprinted return address—mark the Omit check box. To include a return address, make sure the Omit check box is cleared.

6 Observe the Return Address box. Word looks for your return address in the User Information tab of the Options dialog box (Tools, Options). If you want to use a different return address for just this envelope, type and edit the address as needed. If you want to change the return address for future envelopes or labels, see the Tip Sheet on this page.

333 Ellis Rd.
West Caldwell, NY 07006

June 6, 1998

Credit Department
LawnBirds, Inc.
8800 Industrial Way
Emeryville, CA 94608

Dear Sir or Madam:

This letter will confirm that I am disputing the charge highlighted on my latest bill (attached). No way did I order 1000 lawn flamingos. That's 999 too many.

Please research this situation and correct my account. Your attention is greatly appreciated.

Sincerely,

Morton L. Tashjian

Morton L. Tashjian
333 Ellis Rd.
West Caldwell, NY 07006

Credit Department
LawnBirds, Inc.
8800 Industrial Way
Emeryville, CA 94608

How to Choose a Different Envelope Size

To format an envelope correctly, Word has to know what size envelope you plan to use. Word can handle the formatting for a large variety of standard envelope sizes. And if the size you are using is not one that Word recognizes, you simply have to tell Word its dimensions.

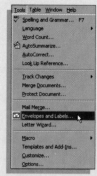

▶ **1** Choose Tools, Envelopes and Labels.

8 Prepare and print the envelope as described on the preceding page.

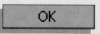

7 Click on OK in the Envelope Options dialog box to return to the Envelopes and Labels dialog box.

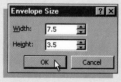

6 In the Width and Height text boxes of the Envelope Size dialog box, type the dimensions of the envelope in inches. Then click on OK.

TIP SHEET

▶ You can perform the steps on this page anytime—not just when you are about to print an envelope. Your envelope size setting remains in effect indefinitely. To change it, simply repeat the steps on this page, specifying a new envelope size in step 5 or 6. In step 8, click the Cancel button to close the Envelopes and Labels dialog box without printing immediately. (Your new size setting will be in effect the next time you print an envelope.)

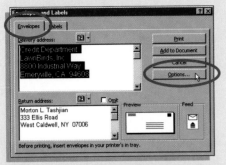

2 In the Envelopes and Labels dialog box, make sure the Envelopes tab is active, and then click on the Options button.

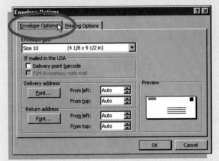

3 In the Envelope Options dialog box, make sure the Envelope Options tab is active.

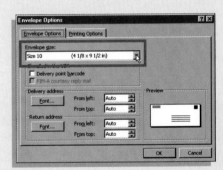

4 Display the Envelope Size drop-down list.

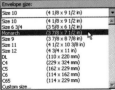

5 If you see the right size, click on it and skip to step 7. Otherwise, click on Custom Size (the last option in the Envelope Size list) and continue with the next step.

How to Prepare and Print Labels

The steps for preparing and printing a single label or a full page of labels with the same address are very similar to those for creating envelopes. However, unlike envelopes, it's quite likely that you'll need to choose a different label type because there are so many commonly used label sizes. If you want to print labels for a mass mailing, you have to use the mail merge feature. (See "How to Print Labels and Envelopes in a Merge" in Chapter 18 for more information.)

TIP SHEET

▸ If you mark the Return Address check box and then modify the address, when you click on the Print button or the Add to Document button, Word asks if you want to save this return address as the default. If you do, click on the Yes button.

▸ Remember, you can change the default return address at any time, not just when you're working with labels. See the Tip Sheet in "How to Prepare and Print an Envelope" earlier in this chapter.

▸ To format the text of your label, select the address in the Labels tab of the Envelopes and Labels dialog box, and then right-click anywhere on the address. Click on Font or Paragraph in the context menu, and make selections in the Font or Paragraph dialog box (see Chapters 9 and 10).

▸ If you have set up a personal address book in Microsoft Outlook (the information management program that ships with MSOffice), you can click on the Insert Address button above the Address box in the Labels and Envelopes dialog box to select an address from your address book.

1 Choose Tools, Envelopes and Labels.

8 To print a single label or a full page of the same label without saving them to disk, make sure the labels are loaded in your printer, and click on the Print button. (This is the *only* available option if you're printing a single label.)

7 If you're printing a full page of the same label and you want to be able to print more copies of the label in the future, click on the New Document button. Word creates the page of labels in a separate document, which you can save to disk, print (make sure the labels are loaded in your printer first), and then close using the standard methods. When you want to print another page of the same labels, simply open the document and print the desired number of copies.

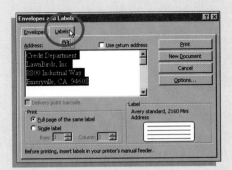

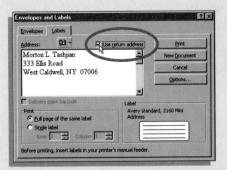

2 Click on the Labels tab if it isn't already active.

3 If Word finds an address in the active document, it displays it in the Address box. Edit or retype the address if necessary. Or, if you want to use your default return address (which Word finds in the User Information tab of the Options dialog box), mark the Use Return Address check box.

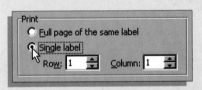

4 To print a single label, mark the Single Label option button, then enter the appropriate values in the Row and Column text boxes to tell Word which label to print on. For example, if the next label on your sheet of labels is the third one in the second column, you'd enter 3 in the Row box and 2 in the Column box. Once you've filled in this information, skip to step 7.

6 At this point, follow the steps on the next page to select the proper label size, then finish with steps 7 and 8 on this page.

5 To print a whole page of labels with the same address on each label, mark the Full Page of the Same Label option button. This option is very useful for printing a page of return address labels.

How to Change the Label Size

The best advice for specifying your label size is to save the box that the labels came in so that you can refer to the product number printed on the box. Word uses product numbers to determine the exact dimensions of all the standard labels; if you select the product number, Word can automatically position the addresses in the right spot on each label. Things get a little trickier if you don't know the product number because you then have to provide Word with the exact measurements of the labels.

TIP SHEET

▶ **The label size you choose remains in effect until you repeat the steps on this page to change it to something else.**

▶ **When you buy labels for a laser printer, make sure the box indicates that they're designed for laser printers. These labels have a special adhesive that prevents the labels from peeling off while inside your printer. (These labels will work fine in ink-jet printers, too.) The labels that are designed to be fed through tractor feeders on dot matrix printers don't work in laser printers.**

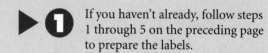

1 If you haven't already, follow steps 1 through 5 on the preceding page to prepare the labels.

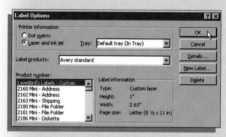

7 If you created a custom label size, you will now see it selected at the top of the Product Number list. Click on OK to close the Label Options dialog box, and then continue with steps 7 and 8 on the preceding page to print the labels.

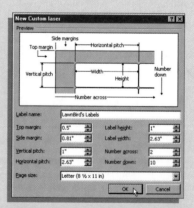

6 Enter a name for your labels in the Label Name text box, and then type the specific measurements of the labels, using the diagram as a guide. (Yes, you have to get out the ruler.) Select the page size in the drop-down list at the bottom of the dialog box, and then click on OK to return to the Label Options dialog box.

2 Click on the Options button to display the Label Options dialog box.

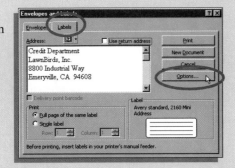

3 Confirm that the appropriate printer type—Laser or Dot Matrix—is selected, and make sure the printer tray you use to hold labels is selected in the Tray list. If you're using standard Avery labels, check that Avery Standard is selected in the Label Products list. If you're using another type of label, select a different option in the list (Avery A4 and A5 Sizes, MACO Standard, or Other).

Mortan L. Tashjian
333 Elis Road
West Caldwell, NY 07006

Mortan L. Tashjian
333 Elis Road
West Caldwell, NY 07006

Mortan L. Tashjian
333 Elis Road
West Caldwell, NY 07006

4 Scroll through the Product Number list and click on the product number of the labels you're using (check the box the labels came in), and then skip to step 7. If you don't know the product number, follow the next two steps.

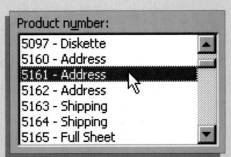

5 Click on the New Label button to display the New Custom Laser (or New Custom Dot Matrix) dialog box.

TRY IT!

Once again, it's time to practice the techniques discussed in the last several chapters. Follow these steps to make a template for creating a customer survey form. As part of this exercise, you'll also create a new style and print an envelope. Don't worry if you don't have the same fonts on your computer as those mentioned in this exercise. You can pick any alternative fonts you'd like from the ones you have available.

Start Word, and then choose File, New to display the New dialog box.

Tropical Fish Emporium
1050 Tenth Street
Philadelphia, PA 19119

We are conducting a survey to make sure we're meeting all of our customers' needs. Please take a few minutes to answer these questions, and then use the attached envelope to mail the survey back to us. Thanks for your help!

1. Did you feel comfortable asking questions?

2. Did the staff answer all your questions?

3. Were you able to find the fish/supplies you were looking for?

4. Do you plan to come back in the future?

5. Do you have any other comments or feedback?

Page 1

Click on the General tab if it isn't already in front, click on the icon for the Blank Document template, click the Template option button, and then click on OK.

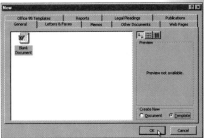

Type the text shown here, pressing Enter once at the end of the first and second lines and three times at the end of the last line.

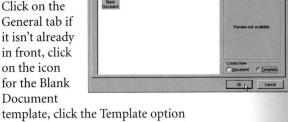

Select the first line (Tropical Fish Emporium). Change its character formatting to Garamond, 16-point, bold.

Select the remaining two lines, and format them as Garamond, 14-point.

Select all three lines (don't include the blank line underneath the address), and click on the Center button on the Standard toolbar.

Keeping the text selected, choose Format, Borders and Shading to display the Borders and Shading dialog box.

Click on the Borders tab if it isn't already active, and click on Custom under Setting.

Continue to next page ▶

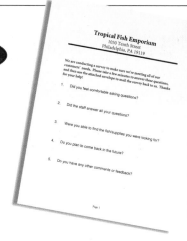

TRY IT!

Continue below

In the Style list, click on a line style you like.

Under Preview, click on the bottom border to apply the border underneath the selected text in your document, and then click on OK.

Choose View, Header and Footer.

Click on the Switch Between Header and Footer button in the Header and Footer toolbar to move into the footer area.

Press Tab once, type **Page** followed by a space, and then click on the Insert Page Number button on the Header and Footer toolbar.

Select the text in the footer area and format it as Garamond, 12-point font.

Click on the Close button on the Header and Footer toolbar.

16

Save the template in the Templates folder with the name TFE Letterhead. Then close the template.

17

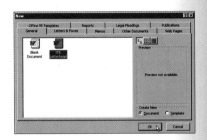

Choose File, New to display the New dialog box. Click on the icon for the TFE Letterhead template in the General tab, keep the Document option button selected, and click on OK to start a document based on the new template.

18

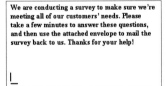

Press Ctrl+End to move the insertion point to the end of the document, and type the paragraph shown here, pressing Enter four times at the end of the paragraph. (Your line breaks will differ from those shown here.) Then select the paragraph and apply a Times New Roman, 12-point, bold font.

19

Press Ctrl+End again, and type the five questions shown here, pressing Enter at the end of each line.

20

Choose Format, Style to display the Style dialog box.

21

Click on the New button to display the New Style dialog box.

22

Enter the name Survey Question in the Name text box, and then mark the Add to Template check box.

Continue to next page ▶

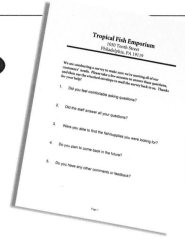

TRY IT!

Continue below

23

Click on the Format button and choose Font.

24

In the Font dialog box, click on the Font tab if it isn't already active, and then choose an Arial, 11-point font. Click on OK to return to the New Style dialog box.

 25

Click on the Format button again, and this time choose Paragraph.

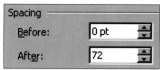
26

In the Paragraph dialog box, click on the Indents and Spacing tab if it isn't already in front, enter 72 in the After box under Spacing, and click on OK. This will add several blank lines under each paragraph formatted with this style.

27

Click the Format button one more time, and this time choose Numbering.

28

In the Bullets and Numbering dialog box, click on the Numbered tab, click on the second format in the top row, and then click on OK.

29

Click on OK again to close the New Style dialog box, and then click on the Close button to close the Style dialog box.

30

Select all five questions (don't include any blank lines above or below the questions), drop down the Style list in the Formatting toolbar, and click on the newly created Survey Question style to apply it to the selected paragraphs.

31

Save the document with the name Survey, print a copy, and then close it. After you issue the Close command, Word asks if you want to save the changes you made to the TFE Letterhead template (since you added a new style to the template). Click on the Yes button.

32

Choose Tools, Envelopes and Labels.

33

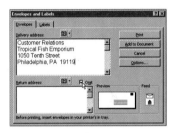

Click on the Envelopes tab if it isn't already in front, type the address shown here in the Delivery Address box, and mark the Omit check box to omit the return address.

34

Optionally, insert an envelope in the appropriate paper tray in your printer, and click on the Print button to print the envelope.

CHAPTER 17

Mail Merge

You can use Word's mail merge feature to create personalized form letters for a mass mailing, or cover letters for a batch of resumes or publicity packages you're sending out. Mail merge automates the process of inserting personal information such as names and addresses into a document you want to send to many people. This chapter explains how to use mail merge to generate form letters. If you also want to print labels or envelopes to go with your letters, see "How to Print Labels and Envelopes in a Merge" in the next chapter.

To set up a mail merge, you need to create two documents: the main document and the data source. The *main document* is the actual document you'll print out, such as a form letter. The *data source* is the list of information, usually names and addresses, that Word plugs into the main document to personalize it for each person on your mailing list.

This chapter guides you through the four main steps of using mail merge: Start (or open) the main document, create (or open) the data source, complete the main document, and merge the information from the data source into the main document. You need to work through these topics in sequence, so find a time when you're alert and have enough time to run through the entire process. A good way to practice is to do a trial merge using a data source that contains only a few names and addresses, and then use your entire mailing list when you're comfortable with the basic procedure.

How to Start the Main Document

Y ou begin the mail merge process by telling Word which document you want to use as your main document. You can either create a new document (as shown on this page) or open an existing document you want to use as your form letter. If you're using a new document, you can type as much or as little of the text as you like at this stage. It's usually simplest to save the blank document without entering any text and move right into creating the data source. Then when you complete the main document, you'll enter both regular text and special merge codes telling Word where to insert each piece of information from the data source.

TIP SHEET

▶ **If you want to use a letter on your disk as your main document, open it, remove all the personal information—such as the name, address, and salutation—and save the document under a new name. Then continue with step 2 on this page. In "How to Complete the Main Document" later in this chapter, you replace the personal information in the letter with merge codes telling Word to pull the names and addresses from the data source.**

▶ **If you plan on running a lot of merges, it's a good idea to create a separate folder to hold your main documents and data source files. In step 2 on this page, double-click on the folder that will contain the new folder (so that it appears in the Save In list at the top of the Save As dialog box), and then click on the Create New Folder button. Type a name for the folder and click on OK. Finally, double-click on the new folder (to display it in the Save In list) before saving the main document.**

▶ **1** Close any open documents, and start a new document. (See the Tip Sheet if you want to use an existing document.)

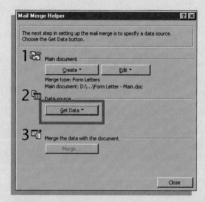

6 Word displays the name and location of the main document under Main Document and activates the Get Data button. You are now ready to perform the next step—creating the data source. Continue on to the next page.

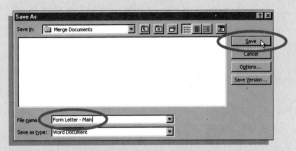

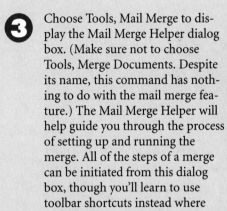

3 Choose Tools, Mail Merge to display the Mail Merge Helper dialog box. (Make sure not to choose Tools, Merge Documents. Despite its name, this command has nothing to do with the mail merge feature.) The Mail Merge Helper will help guide you through the process of setting up and running the merge. All of the steps of a merge can be initiated from this dialog box, though you'll learn to use toolbar shortcuts instead where appropriate.

2 Save the blank document to disk. It's helpful to choose a name that will remind you that this is a main document, such as *Form Letter-Main* in this example. That way, when you're looking at a list of files on your disk, you'll be able to easily recognize this document as one that's designed for use in a mail merge. Select a folder for the document, and click on the Save button.

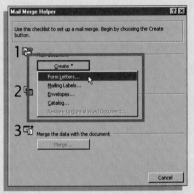

4 Under Main Document, click on the Create button. Word displays a list of the different types of main documents you can create. Click on Form Letters. (In the next chapter, you learn how to use the Mailing Labels and Envelopes options to print labels or envelopes to go with your form letters.)

5 Word asks what document you want to use as your main document. Since you've already started (or opened) yours, click on the Active Window button.

How to Create the Data Source

Because a data source is a simple database, you need to understand two database-related terms to work with it: record and field. A *record* is all the information about one person in your data source. If you have 50 people's names and addresses in your data source, for example, it would contain 50 records. A *field* is one category of information within each record. Typical fields include first name, last name, company, address, city, state, zip code, and so on. The first part of creating a data source is to define what fields you want to use; the second part is to enter the data. Follow the steps on this page and the next to create your data source.

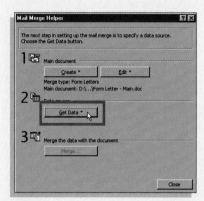

▶ ❶ If you haven't done so yet, follow the steps in "How to Start the Main Document" on the preceding page. Then click on the Get Data button in the Mail Merge Helper dialog box.

❽ In the example shown in step 7, the list of fields has been modified to include the following fields: FirstName, LastName, Company, Address1, City, State, PostalCode, and Salutation. If many of your addresses include building names or suite numbers, you may want to keep the Address2 field. The Salutation field is a nice one to add because it lets you use a name other than the first name or the last name after *Dear* in the salutation of a form letter.

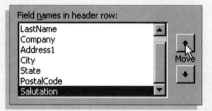

❼ To change the position of a field in the list, click on the field, then use the Move arrows to move it up or down the list. The field order in the Field Names in Header Row list doesn't affect the order in which you can place fields in your main document. Positioning them in a logical order now simply helps when you enter the actual data a little bit later on.

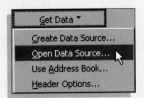

2 Word lets you create a new data source or open one from disk. If you already have a Word data source on disk, choose Open Data Source, select the file from the Open Data Source dialog box, and click on the Open button. Click on the Edit Main Document button when prompted, and skip to "How to Complete the Main Document" later in this chapter.

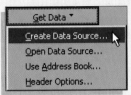

3 If you're creating your data source from scratch, choose Create Data Source to display the Create Data Source dialog box (shown in the middle of the page), and continue with the next step.

4 The Create Data Source dialog box is the place where you define which fields you want to use in your data source. Word displays a list of the most typical fields under Field Names in Header Row. Your job is to remove the fields you don't need, add any new ones you want to use, and optionally change the order of the fields in the list.

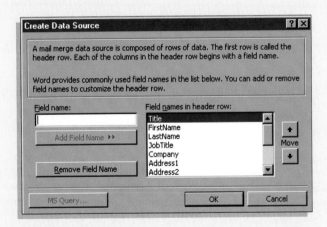

5 To remove a field, click on it, and then click on the Remove Field Name button.

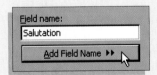

6 To add a field, type the new field name in the Field Name text box (if a field name is currently in the box, select it and type over it), and click on the Add Field Name button. Word adds the new field to the bottom of the list. No spaces are allowed in field names. Also, it's fine to include fields that you want for reference purposes but don't intend to actually use in form letters, such as phone numbers or e-mail addresses.

Continue to next page ▶

How to Create the Data Source

(Continued)

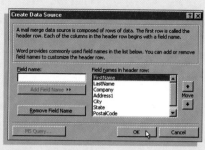

▶ **9** When you've finished defining your fields, click on the OK button.

▶ **If you already have a database of names and addresses in another database program, such as Access, Paradox, or FoxPro, you may be able to use that file as your data source. In step 2 on this page, choose Open Data Source, and then in the Open Data Source dialog box, display the Files of Type list and click on the appropriate file format. Locate and select your database file, and then click on the Open button.**

▶ **The easiest way to edit the data source in the future is to open it *through* the main document. First open the main document (File, Open). Then click on the Edit Data Source button at the far right end of the Mail Merge toolbar to display the Data Form. Make your revisions to the records, and then click on OK to close the Data Form. Save the main document, and click on Yes when Word asks if you want to save the data source attached to the main document.**

OK

16 When you're finished entering records, click on the OK button to close the Data Form. Congratulations! You've completed the most difficult part of the mail merge process. Proceed to the next page to complete the main document.

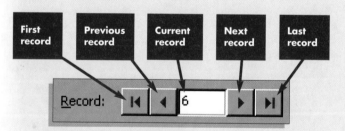

15 Word indicates which record you are on at the bottom of the Data Form. If you need to edit a previous record, you can use the red arrows to bring it into view. To delete a record, display it and then click on the Delete button.

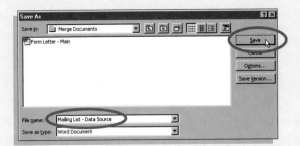

10 Word displays the Save As dialog box because it needs to save the data source before allowing you to start entering records. It's a good idea to choose a file name—such as Mailing List–Data Source in this example—that clearly indicates the document is a data source file. Select a folder for the document, and then click on the Save button.

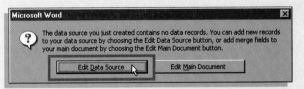

11 Word displays a message box informing you that your data source doesn't yet have any records in it. Click on the Edit Data Source button to start adding the actual data. Depending on how many people are in your mailing list, this could be a time-consuming process. Luckily, you only have to do it once. (When you create other main documents in the future, you can use this same data source with them—see step 2 on the previous page.)

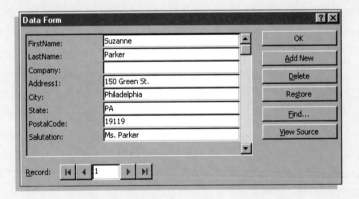

12 Word displays the Data Form dialog box (shown in the middle of the page), which functions as an intermediary between you and the table Word uses behind the scenes to store your data source. The dialog box contains a text box for each field you defined in steps 5 and 6 on the previous page. Type the data for the first record, pressing Tab to move to the next field (or Shift+Tab to move to or the previous field). The order in which you enter the records doesn't matter. (In the next chapter, you learn how to change the sort order.)

13 When you've finished typing the first record, click on the Add New button. Be careful not to click on the OK button at this point. If you do, Word closes the Data Form and displays the main document. To return to the Data Form if you closed it accidentally, click on the Edit Data Source button at the far right edge of the Mail Merge toolbar just underneath the Formatting toolbar.

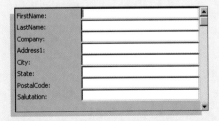

14 When you click on Add New, Word empties the text boxes in the Data Form to let you enter the second record. Continue typing new records and pressing Add New in between each one.

How to Complete the Main Document

his is the fun part of setting up a mail merge. If your main document is blank at this point, you need to both type and format the text and insert the merge codes. If the main document already contains the text and formatting, you need only insert the codes (see steps 4 through 7).

1 If you haven't done so yet, follow the steps in the first two topics of this chapter. After you close the Data Form in the last step on the preceding page, Word displays the main document (named Form Letter-Main in this example).

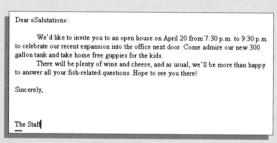

8 Type the body of the letter and the closing. Then save the main document and go on to the next page, which describes the final step in the mail merge process, running the merge.

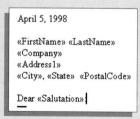

7 Repeat steps 4 and 5 to insert the remaining fields for the address block, pressing Enter and adding spaces and commas where necessary. If you have a Salutation field, insert it after the word *Dear*, and follow it with a colon or a comma. (You can, of course, also use some combination of other fields for the salutation—such as Title and LastName, or FirstName.)

2 The Mail Merge toolbar appears at the top of the document window under the Formatting toolbar. You'll use a few of the Mail Merge toolbar buttons in this and the next page.

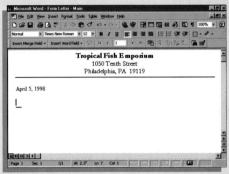

Tropical Fish Emporium

1050 Tenth Street
Philadelphia, PA 19119

April 5, 1998

<<FirstName>> <<LastName>>
<<Company>>
<<Address1>>
<<City>>, <<State>> <<PostalCode>>

Dear <<Salutation>>:

We'd like to invite you to an open house on April 20 from 7:30 p.m. to 9:30 p.m. to celebrate our recent expansion into the office next door. Come admire our new 300 gallon tank and take home free guppies for the kids.
There will be plenty of wine and cheese, and as usual, we'll be more than happy to answer all your fish-related questions. Hope to see you there!

Sincerely,

The Staff

3 Type and format the text you want to include above the recipient's address. If you like, you can insert the date automatically with the Insert, Date and Time command (see Chapter 8).

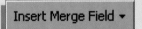

4 Place the insertion point where you want the first line of the address block to begin, and click on the Insert Merge Field button at the left end of the Mail Merge toolbar.

6 Word inserts the field in the main document. Note that Word indicates merge codes by surrounding them with chevron brackets.

5 Word displays a list of all the fields in the attached data source. Click on the first field for the address block (FirstName in this example).

How to Run the Merge

In this final step of the merge process, Word merges the main document with the data source. The product of the merge is a document called *Form Letters1* that contains all the merged letters. Before you run the merge, it's a good idea to follow steps 2 through 5 on this page to confirm that everything is set up properly.

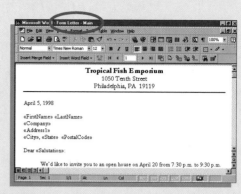

1 If you haven't already done so, follow the steps on the preceding pages in this chapter. You should now have your completed (and saved) main document on screen.

7 When you're ready, print the form letters using the standard methods for printing a document. Then close the Form Letters document without saving it (you don't normally need to save the merged letters), and close the main document. If Word asks whether you want to save the data source attached to the main document, click on the Yes button to save any revisions you've made to the data source.

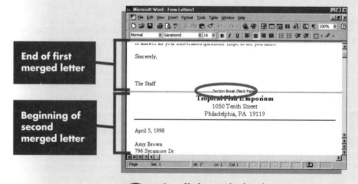

End of first merged letter

Beginning of second merged letter

6 Scroll through the document to view the letters. Word separates the letters with next page section breaks, so each letter begins on a new page.

2 To check that the merge codes are in the proper places and that the information in the data source is entered correctly, click on the View Merged Data button on the Mail Merge toolbar.

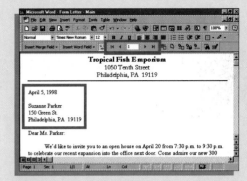

3 Word displays the data from the first record of your data source in place of the merge codes. Notice that since this record doesn't contain a company name, Word automatically closed up the blank line. Use the red arrows to check the data from a few more records. If you spot a problem, either edit the main document itself or edit the data source (see the Tip Sheet in "How to Complete the Main Document" on the previous page).

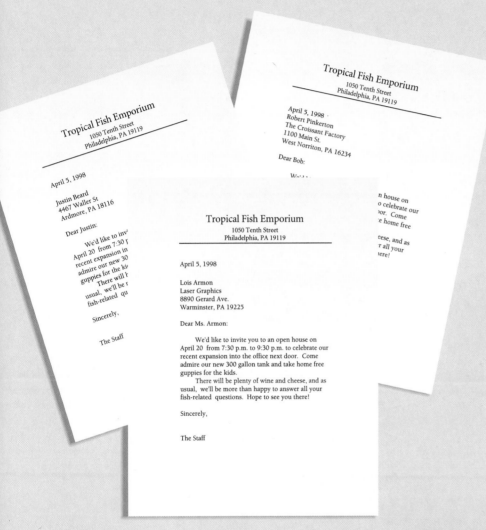

4 When you're satisfied that everything is set up properly, click on the View Merged Data button again to turn it off. Then click on the Merge to New Document button on the Mail Merge toolbar. (The Merge to Printer button also runs a merge, but it sends the merged documents directly to the printer, without displaying them on your screen first.)

5 Depending on how many records are in your data source, Word could take anywhere from a few seconds to several minutes to merge the data. When it's finished, it displays the merged letters on your screen in a document named *Form Letters1*.

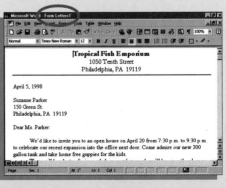

CHAPTER 18

Advanced Mail Merge

 In the last chapter, you learned the basic skills required to prepare and merge a form letter. Here, you have a chance to broaden your mail-merge repertoire further: You learn how to merge envelopes and labels, how to sort merged records in a particular order, and how to merge only a selected group of records in your data source.

Chances are that you usually need to print labels or envelopes to go with your form letters. When you merge addresses onto labels or envelopes, the four basic steps of performing a mail merge stay the same (see Chapter 17). However, two aspects of the process are slightly different: The main document is a label or an envelope instead of a form letter, and it's easier to merge labels and envelopes from the Mail Merge Helper dialog box than from the Mail Merge toolbar in the main document.

If you want to print your merged documents in a particular order, you have to define a sort order for the records in your data source before you run the merge. Word makes it easy to sort using up to three fields. So you could, for example, sort your records in zip code order, and within zip code by last name.

Finally, you can define a *filter* for your data source to tell Word to merge some of the records in your data source, but not others. If you want to send a form letter to clients who live in San Francisco, for example, you can tell Word to merge only those addresses in a client mailing list that contain *San Francisco* in the city field.

How to Print Labels and Envelopes in a Merge

If you haven't yet, work through Chapter 17 now to create the data source you want to use, and if you're also creating a form letter, merge and print the letters. Then follow the steps on this page and the next to print the labels or envelopes. If you don't have an envelope tray on your printer that lets you feed envelopes automatically, it will be much simpler for you to print labels.

▶ **1** Close all open documents and start a new document. This document will be your main document (either a page of labels or an envelope). Save it and give it a descriptive name such as Labels-Main or Envelopes-Main. Then choose Tools, Mail Merge to display the Mail Merge Helper dialog box.

8 Word displays the Create Label dialog box to let you insert the merge codes telling Word where to place the information from the data source. This process is very similar to inserting the codes in a form letter (see "How to Complete the Main Document" in Chapter 17). Begin by clicking the Insert Merge Field button, and click on the first field of the address block.

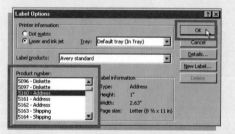

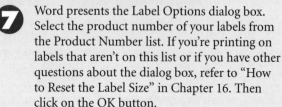

7 Word presents the Label Options dialog box. Select the product number of your labels from the Product Number list. If you're printing on labels that aren't on this list or if you have other questions about the dialog box, refer to "How to Reset the Label Size" in Chapter 16. Then click on the OK button.

2 Click on the Create button under Main Document, and choose Mailing Labels or Envelopes.

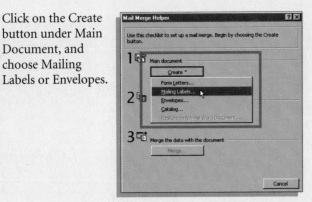

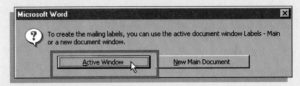

3 Word asks what document you want to use as your main document. Since you've already started the main document, click on the Active Window button.

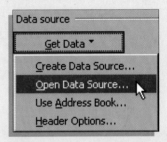

4 Click on the Get Data button, and then click on Open Data Source.

Tropical Fish Emporium
1050 Tenth Street
Philadelphia, PA 19119

<<FirstName>> <<LastName>>
<<Company>>
<<Address1>>
<<City>>, <<State>> <<PostalCode>>

5 In the Open Data Source dialog box, select the folder that contains your data source, click on the file name, and click on the Open button.

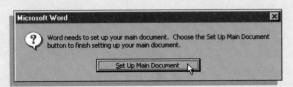

6 When Word informs you that it needs to set up the main document, click on the Set Up Main Document button. If you're merging labels, follow steps 7 through 10, and then skip to step 13. If you're merging envelopes, skip to step 11.

Continue to next page ▶

How to Print Labels and Envelopes in a Merge

(Continued)

▶ If you notice any problems with the merged labels or envelopes, close the Labels or Envelopes document without saving it and fix the problem in either the main document or the data source. The main document will be open after you run the merge (use the Window menu if necessary to switch to it). To edit the data source, click on the Edit Data Source button in the Mail Merge toolbar in the main document.

▶ To omit the return address in the merged envelopes, follow these steps:

  ▶ Before you run the merge, choose Tools, Options.

  ▶ Click on the User Information tab.

  ▶ Delete the address under Mailing Address.

  ▶ Click on OK.

  ▶ After you've merged and printed the envelopes, retype the address in the User Information tab.

▶ You don't have to repeat the steps on this page each time you want to print the same labels or envelopes in the future. After you've run the merge and printed the labels or envelopes, save and close the main document. (If you don't see the main document, use the Window menu to switch to it.) When you want to print the labels or envelopes, open the main document and click on the Merge to New Document button in the Mail Merge toolbar to run the merge, then print.

 Word inserts the field in the Sample Label area.

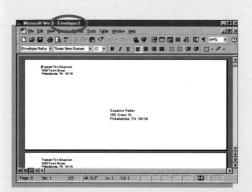

 Word merges the envelopes into a document named *Envelopes1*, shown here in Page Layout view. Scroll through the envelopes to make sure there aren't any problems, make sure your envelopes are properly loaded in your printer, and then print using the standard methods. You can close this document without saving it.

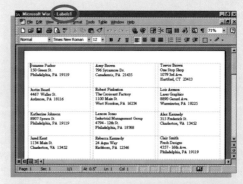

 Word merges the labels into a document titled *Labels1*, shown here in Page Layout view. Scroll through the labels to view them if you'd like. Make sure the label paper is in the proper paper tray, and print the labels using one of the standard printing methods (see Chapter 2). You can then close this document without saving it.

10 Insert the remainder of the fields, adding commas and spaces and pressing Enter as necessary, and click on OK. Then skip to step 13.

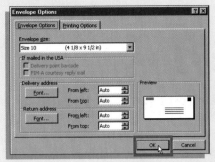

11 After you click on the Set Up Main Document location in Step 6 on the previous page, Word displays the Envelope Options dialog box. Change the envelope size if necessary (see "How to Reset the Envelope Size" in Chapter 16), and then click on OK.

12 Word displays the Envelope Address dialog box to let you insert the merge codes in the envelope. Use the Insert Merge Field button to insert all the fields in their proper positions, pressing Enter at the end of the lines, and inserting commas and spaces as necessary. Then click on OK.

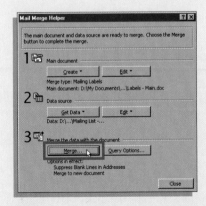

14 Make sure the option under Merge To is set to New Document, and click on the Merge button to run the merge. (See the remaining two topics in this chapter to learn how to use this dialog box to change the order in which the records are sorted, or to select only certain records to merge.) If you are merging labels, go to the next step. If you're merging envelopes, go to step 16.

13 Word redisplays the Mail Merge Helper dialog box, and the Merge button is now active. Click on the Merge button to display the Merge dialog box.

How to Sort Records in a Merge

Sometimes you have to print out your merged documents in a particular order. For example, you might want to print your form letters in alphabetical order, or if you're doing a bulk mailing, you might need to print labels in zip code order. Word allows you to sort the records in the data source before running the merge. The example on this page shows labels, but you can use the same technique for sorting envelopes or form letters.

▶ **The options you set in the Query Options dialog box remain in effect until you clear them. So if you establish a particular sort order and then add records to the data source, Word automatically sorts the new records into the existing sort order. To clear the sort order, display the Query Options dialog box (see step 2 on this page) and click on the Clear All button. You can now repeat steps 4 through 7 to define a different sort order, if desired.**

▶ **1** Begin by following steps 1 through 13 in the previous topic, "How to Print Labels or Envelopes in a Merge." (If you want to sort records when merging a form letter, open the form letter main document, and click on the Mail Merge button in the Mail Merge toolbar.) The Merge dialog box should now be displayed on your screen.

Justin Beard 4467 Waller St. Ardmore, PA 18116	Teresa Robinson The Pizza Factory 340 Pleasant Valley Rd. Ardmore, PA 18116	Scott Stevens 8907 - 16th Ave. Ardmore, PA 18115
Darin Levin Burnham Fish and Supplies 345 Main St. Bethlehem, PA 23419	Amy Brown 796 Sycamore Dr. Canadensis, PA 21435	Kiana Malik Zephyr Graphics 176 Victoria Place Canadensis, PA 21435
Alex Kennedy 315 Frederick St. Charleston, VA 13452	Jared Kent 1134 Main St. Charleston, VA 13452	Trevor Brown One Stop Shop 1079 3rd Ave. Hartford, CT 23413
Elaine Kahn 9273 - 29th St. Hartford, CT 39044	Katherine Johnson 8907 Spruce St. Philadelphia, PA 19119	Lenora Jones Industrial Management Group 4794 - 12th St. Philadelphia, PA 18768

 The merged documents are sorted in the order you defined (in this case, the labels are sorted first by city, then by last name, and then by first name).

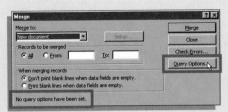

2 Notice that Word displays the message *No Query Options have been set* at the bottom of the dialog box. This message will change as soon as you define a sort order. Click on the Query Options button to display the Query Options dialog box.

3 Click on the Sort Records tab if it isn't already in front.

4 Display the Sort By list, and click on the field you want to use for the primary sort. If you don't want to refine the sort any more than this, skip to step 7.

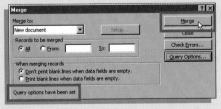

6 Word now displays the message *Query Options have been set.* Click on the Merge button to perform the merge.

5 To further refine the sort, display the first Then By list, and select the field you want to sort on whenever Word finds more than one record containing the same value in the first sort field. In this example, Word will sort all the records containing the same city by last name. Optionally, use the second Then By list to define a third field to sort on. Here, Word will sort within the same last name by first name. When you're finished, click on the OK button to return to the Merge dialog box.

How to Merge a Selected Group of Records

At times you may want to print form letters, labels, or envelopes for some of the people in your data source, but not others. Word lets you filter the records based on rules that you define, and then it merges only those records that conform to your rules. The example on this page shows labels, but you can just as easily use these steps to establish a filter for envelopes or form letters.

TIP SHEET

▶ **The options you set in the Query Options dialog box remain in effect until you clear them. This is important to remember if you've set filter options, because until you clear the options (by clicking the Clear All button in the Query Options dialog box) you won't be able to merge all of the records in the data source.**

▶ **Many of the choices in the Comparison list are only useful number or date fields. For example, if you have a salary field and you want to send a letter to only those employees who earn over a particular amount, you would select the salary field in step 4, select Greater Than in the Comparison list, and then type the cut-off salary in the Compare To box.**

▶ **If you like, you can use additional rows in the Filter tab of the Query Options dialog box to set up additional rules. You have to connect multiple rules by selecting And or Or from the drop-down list at the left edge of the dialog box. If you aren't sure how to use And and Or operators, use the Office Assistant to search on-line help for topics related to "rules for selecting data records" (see Chapter 3).**

▶ **1** Begin by following steps 1 through 13 in "How to Print Labels or Envelopes in a Merge." (If you want to filter records when merging a form letter, open the form letter main document, and click on the Mail Merge button in the Mail Merge toolbar.) The Merge dialog box should now be displayed on your screen.

Word merged only Philadelphia addresses.

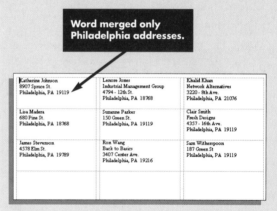

8 Word merges only the records that match the rule you defined.

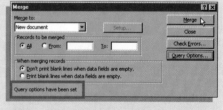

7 The message at the bottom of the dialog box now says *Query Options have been set*. Click on the Merge button to run the merge.

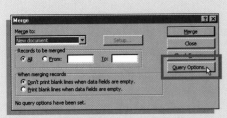

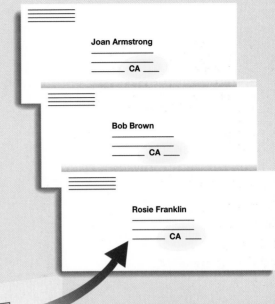

② Word displays the message *No Query Options have been set* at the bottom of the dialog box. This message will change as soon as you define a filter. Click on the Query Options button to display the Query Options dialog box.

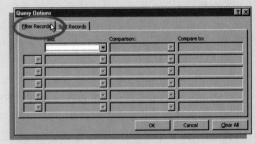

③ Click on the Filter Records tab if it isn't already in front.

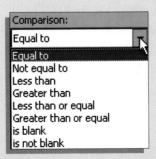

④ Display the Field list, and click on the field you want to use to filter the records.

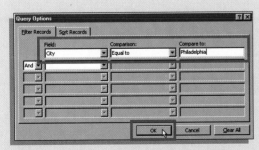

⑥ In the Compare To box, enter the value you are looking for. In this example, Word will only merge records that contain *Philadelphia* in the City field. Click on the OK button to return to the Merge dialog box.

⑤ If necessary, display the list of choices under Comparison. If you want to look for records that contain one particular value in a field (94117 in the PostalCode field or New York in the City field, for example) you can leave this option set to Equal To.

CHAPTER 19

Graphics

 You don't have to be a graphics wizard or an artistic genius to use graphics effectively in your documents. With a few simple commands, you can add a company logo to your letterhead, place a fancy divider between two parts of the page, or liven up a flyer with a picture or two.

If you like, you can use the 2,000-plus clip art images that come on the Microsoft Office CD in your Word documents or Web pages (see the next chapter). If prefab art is not your style, you can also use graphics you've created yourself, images you've downloaded from the Web, photographs you've scanned, and so on. Word can handle graphic images in all the standard formats, including BMP, EPS, TIF, PCX, and WMF. It also recognizes graphics in the GIF and JPEG formats, which are used widely on the World Wide Web. In fact, if you insert a graphic in a Web page that is not a GIF or JPEG file, Word automatically converts it to a GIF for you (more about Web pages in the next chapter).

In this chapter, you first learn how to insert a graphic in your document, and then you'll learn how to change its position and size. Finally, you get a brief introduction to the many ways you can format a graphic image once it's in your document.

How to Insert a Graphic

It only takes a mouse click or two to insert a graphic. Once it's in the document, however, you'll almost always have to adjust its size, position, and so on. So after you finish the steps on this page, go ahead and review the remaining two topics in this chapter—you'll then be able to fine-tune the way the graphic fits into your document. This page describes how to insert the clip art images that come on the Microsoft Office CD. See the Tip Sheet if you have other graphic images you want to use.

1 Move the insertion point to the approximate position where you want to insert the graphic.

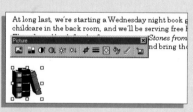

8 Word switches to Page Layout view and inserts the image in your document. It also displays the Picture toolbar, which contains buttons for helping you work with images. The white squares surrounding the image (called *sizing handles*) indicate that it's currently selected. You can select a graphic image at any time by clicking on it. If you want to delete an image, select it and press the Delete key.

2 Place the Microsoft Office CD in the drive. (If you installed Word from floppy disks, you need to install the clip art on your hard disk to access it.) Choose Insert, Picture, Clip Art to display the Microsoft Clip Gallery 3.0 dialog box.

Click on different categories to view the images they contain.

3 The Clip Gallery contains tabs for clip art, pictures (photographic images), sounds, and videos. The examples in this chapter use clip art, but you could use similar methods to work with other types of clips as well. In the Clip Art tab, click on the various categories to browse the available images. When you click on an image (the donkey in this example), the keywords associated with the image appear at the bottom of the dialog box (see steps 5 through 7).

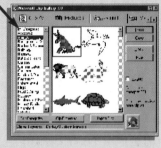

4 If you want to see the images more clearly, mark the Magnify check box. Now when you click on an image, it enlarges and its name appears under the clip. If you find an image you want to use, select it and click on the Insert button, and then skip to step 8. If you want to search for a particular type of image, continue to the next step.

5 If you know what type of image you are looking for, you can search for it by keyword. This is often faster than browsing category by category. Start by clicking on the Find button.

7 Word searches the CD for images matching the criteria you specified, and then displays the images it finds in a category called Results of Last Find. Click on the image you want to use, and click on the Insert button.

6 In the Find Clip dialog box, type a keyword to describe what you're looking for. In this example, Word will look for images related to books. Keywords aren't related to the actual file names of the images. If you want to search for text contained in the actual file names, use the File Name Containing text box. To restrict the search to graphics of a particular format (WMF, GIF, JPEG, and so on) specify the type in the Clip Type drop-down list. When you've made your choices, click on the Find Now button to start the search.

How to Move and Resize a Graphic

Word lets you quickly move or change the size of a graphic by dragging with the mouse. However, if you need to place the graphic in an exact location or make it an exact size, you might find it easier to use the Format Picture dialog box. Both methods are described on this page; you will probably end up using a combination of the two.

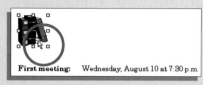

1 Point anywhere inside the graphic; the mouse pointer changes to show a four-headed arrow. When you see this mouse pointer, you can drag to move the graphic around the document.

▶ **Word also supplies a Drawing toolbar, which contains additional buttons for working with graphic images. To display the Drawing toolbar, click the Drawing button on the Standard toolbar (or choose View, Toolbars, Drawing).**

▶ **The Position tab of the Format Picture dialog box contains three check boxes (see step 6) that you will probably find useful. To keep an image in the same position on the page regardless of whether you adjust the surrounding text, clear the Move Object with Text check box. If you want a graphic to always stay on the same page as the adjoining paragraph, mark the Lock Anchor check box. Finally, keep the default option Float Over Text marked if you want to be able to "float" the image over or under the text in your document.**

7 To specify an exact size for your image, click on the Size tab. Under Size and Rotate, type the desired height and width in inches. If you want to resize the image proportionally, leave the Lock Aspect Ratio check box marked. With this option marked, you only have to change the height or the width, and Word will automatically adjust the other measurement. You can also specify a size relative to the original image size by changing the percentages under Scale.

2 Drag the graphic, and release the mouse when it is in the desired location.

3 To resize a graphic, select it and then point to one of the sizing handles (the small white squares). The mouse pointer changes to a double-headed arrow. If you want the graphic to be resized proportionally, drag a corner handle—if you use one of the side handles, the image will get skewed when you resize it.

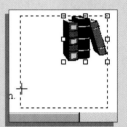

4 Drag until the graphic is the right size, and then release the mouse.

5 If you want to specify an exact location or size for an image, select it, and then click the Format Picture button on the Picture toolbar to display the Format Picture dialog box. (If you don't see the Picture toolbar, right-click on the graphic and choose Show Picture Toolbar). Alternatively, you can display the Format Picture dialog box by right-clicking on the graphic and choosing Format Picture from the context menu.

6 Click on Position tab to specify an exact location for the graphic. Under Position on Page, enter a horizontal and/or vertical measurement in inches. If necessary, you can change the settings in the From drop-down lists to specify the point from which you want to position the left (horizontal) and top (vertical) edges of the image.

How to Format a Graphic

Word lets you format graphic images in many different ways (insert an image, display the Drawing and Picture toolbars, and experiment!). On this page, you learn three of the most common adjustments. First, you find out how to change the way the text wraps around the image. Next, you learn how to lighten an image's coloring to turn it into a watermark, and finally, you learn how to place a graphic image behind your text.

1 By default, Word doesn't allow text to wrap around graphic images. In many cases, such as when you're placing a picture in a news article, you need to change this setting to let the text wrap around one or both sides of the image. In this example, the First meeting and Location text block should wrap around the left side of the image, instead of shifting down below it.

7 If you want to lighten an image's colors so that you can easily read the text placed on top of it, select the image, choose the Image Control button in Picture toolbar, and click on Watermark. In the sample document on this page, the fern image was converted to a watermark after it was sent behind the text.

TIP SHEET

▶ **To read descriptions of the various options in the Wrapping tab of the Format Picture dialog box (see step 3), click the small question-mark button in the upper-right corner of the dialog box, and then click on the option you are curious about. Word displays a ScreenTip with a concise explanation of the option. (Click again to hide the ScreenTip.)**

2 To change the way your text wraps around an image, first select the image, and then choose Format Picture button from the Picture toolbar (or right-click on the graphic and choose Format Picture from the context menu) to display the Format Picture dialog box.

3 Click on the Wrapping tab. Under Wrapping Style, click the type of wrapping you want. In this example, the Square option will make the text wrap in a square shape around the image. Under Wrap To, click an option to specify which sides of the image the text should wrap around. Here, choosing Left will allow the text to flow down the left side of the image. Optionally increase or decrease the distance between the text and the image under Distance from Text, and then click on OK.

COME JOIN!
THE FERNWOOD COFFEEHOUSE
BOOK GROUP

At long last, we're starting a Wednesday night book group. There will be childcare in the back room, and we'll be serving free house coffee and treats. The selected book for the first meeting is *Stones from the River*, by Ursula Hegi. Please read it before the meeting, and bring thoughts for the discussion and ideas for future books.

First meeting: Wednesday, August 10 at 7:30 p.m.

Location: The Fernwood Coffeehouse
158 River Road in Pine Grove

If you have any questions or would like to help organize future meetings, please call Scott at 746-6645.

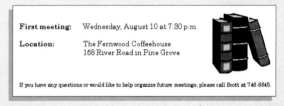

4 The text shifts up and wraps to the left of the image.

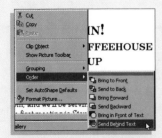

6 To place an image behind your text, first follow steps 2 and 3 to set the image's wrapping style to None, and then drag the image over the text. Next, right-click on the image, and choose Order, Send Behind Text from the context menu. The fern image in the sample document on this page is placed behind the heading.

5 If you want to place an image on top of your text, first follow steps 2 and 3 and choose a Wrapping style of None. Then simply drag the image over the text.

CHAPTER 20

Word and the Internet

 This final chapter introduces you to Word 97's new Internet-related features. If you are unfamiliar with the Internet and the World Wide Web, you might want to do a bit of background reading before diving into this material. A great place to start is *How to Use the Internet, Third Edition*, published by Ziff-Davis Press.

If you don't have time to study up on the Internet, here is a crash course in concepts and terms: The Internet is a global network of interconnected computers. The most popular part of the Internet is the World Wide Web, a vast collection of interlinked documents. Computers that store Web documents are usually called *Web sites*, but because the Web uses a protocol called HTTP to transfer documents, Word refers to Web sites as *HTTP locations*.

Your company may also have an *intranet*, a private network that supports HTTP. The documents stored on an intranet Web site are only visible to company employees.

To explore most of the topics in this chapter, you need to have an Internet connection—and/or a connection to a company intranet—and a browser such as Netscape or Internet Explorer. (A *browser* is a program that lets you access the World Wide Web.) And if you want to create Web pages, your installation of Office 97 should include the Web page authoring tools. If it doesn't, you need to rerun the Microsoft Office 97 setup program to add them. (If you have questions, ask your friendly neighborhood computer guru or system administrator to assist you.)

How to View Documents on the Web or an Intranet

The most common way to view documents on the Web or an intranet is to use a browser such as Netscape or Internet Explorer. Although browsers do a great job of displaying actual Web pages, they usually need add-on software to properly display Word documents. In contrast, Word now lets you view both Word documents and Web pages stored on Web sites (or on your intranet). Word can either display Web pages directly in the Word window, or it can launch your browser (Netscape, in these examples), which then opens the page for you. It always displays Word documents directly in the Word window.

TIP SHEET

▶ **Web pages don't always display properly in the Word window. If you want to view a page with complex graphics and formatting, it's better to enter the URL in the Web toolbar than in the Open dialog box, so that Word will display the page in your browser.**

▶ **Clicking on the Search the Web button in the Web toolbar displays the search page at Microsoft's Web site. If you want the button to jump to a different search service instead—such as Yahoo! (http://www.yahoo.com) or Infoseek (http://www.infoseek.com)—first display the desired site in Word (see step 7), then choose Go, Set Search Page from the Web toolbar, and click on Yes in the Set Search Page dialog box.**

▶ **Clicking on the Start Page button in the Web toolbar takes you to Microsoft's home page. If you want to change the start page, first display the desired page in Word (see step 7), then choose Go, Set Start Page from the Web toolbar, and click on Yes in the Set Start Page dialog box.**

1 If you want Word to open a Web page in your browser, first display the Web toolbar by clicking on the Web Toolbar button in the Standard toolbar. (To later hide the Web toolbar, just click on the same button again.)

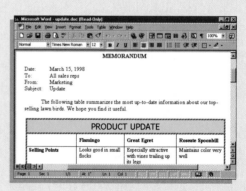

8 Word loads the document in the Word window. Word displays [Read Only] in the title bar because you can't edit documents opened from Web sites (either on the World Wide Web or an intranet). If you want to revise the document, save it onto your own computer or onto a network drive first, and then make your changes to the new copy.

Type the URL here and press Enter.

2 Type the address (also called the URL) for the Web page in the Address box on the right side of the Web toolbar. You can omit the standard http:// at the beginning of the address and the trailing slash. For example, the full address for this Web site is http://www.exoticbird.com/, but you only need to type www.exoticbird.com. If you don't specify the actual name of a Web page (Web page names end with the extension .htm or .html), Word looks for the default page at the site. This URL points to Those Majestic Macaws, a Web site for people who love macaws.

3 Press Enter after you've typed in the URL. After a moment, your default browser loads and jumps to the URL you typed. (If you were not online when you pressed Enter, you'll first see the Connect To dialog box. Enter your user name and password for your Internet account, and click on the Connect button.)

A Web page displayed in Word

4 Continue browsing Web pages in your browser if you like. When you are ready to go back to Word, disconnect from your Internet service provider (if you don't plan to go back to your browser soon), and click on the taskbar button for Microsoft Word at the bottom of the screen.

5 Word loads a new copy of your browser every time you enter a URL in the Web toolbar, even if your browser is already open. To avoid loading extra copies of your browser, check whether the browser is already open before entering the URL in the Web toolbar. If it is, click on its taskbar button and enter the URL in the browser window instead of in Word.

7 If you want to load a Web page or a Word document directly in the Word window, click on the Open button in the Standard toolbar (or choose File, Open). Type the URL in the File Name text box, and then click on the Open button. In this example, the URL points to a Word document named update.doc that's stored on the company intranet.

6 After you have typed the URL and pressed Enter, you can click on the Stop Current Jump button if you want to stop loading the Web page.

How to Create Hyperlinks

A hyperlink is a piece of text or a graphic that you can click on to jump to another location. You can add hyperlinks to Word documents, as shown on this page, or to Web pages (see "How to Modify a Web Page" later in the chapter). The destination of a hyperlink can be another document on your network—either a Word document or a document created in another program—or a Web page. You can even link to a specific location in a document. Keep in mind that hyperlinks are only useful if you're distributing your document electronically and expect people to read your document on screen. And make sure that your readers can access the documents you link to. For example, if you link to a document on your local hard drive (C:) instead of a network drive, other people on your network won't be able to jump to the document.

1 Select the words (or the graphic image) that you want to form the hyperlink.

8 By default, Word automatically formats URLs you type in your documents as hyperlinks as soon as you finish typing the URL and press the spacebar.

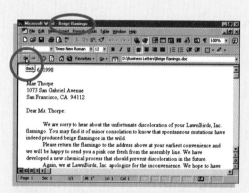

7 Word displays the destination document. If the destination is a Web page, Word displays the page in your browser. To go back to the document containing the hyperlink, click on the Back button in the Web toolbar, or if you're in your browser or another program that isn't part of Microsoft Office 97, click on the Microsoft Word taskbar button. (In Microsoft Office 97 programs, you can display the Web Toolbar at any time by clicking on the Web Toolbar button in the Standard toolbar.)

TIP SHEET

▶ When you click on a hyperlink that points to a document that was created in a program other than Word, Word first loads the program, and then opens the document within it. If the program is part of Office 97 (Excel, Access, or PowerPoint), you'll see the Web toolbar at the top of the program window.

▶ To delete a hyperlink, right-click on the link and point to Hyperlink in the context menu. Click on Select Hyperlink, and then press the Delete key.

2 Click on the Insert Hyperlink button in the Standard toolbar (or choose Insert, Hyperlink).

3 In the Insert Hyperlink dialog box, enter the destination for your link in the Link to File or URL text box. If the destination is a URL, type it directly into the text box, click on OK, and skip to step 6. If the destination is a document on your network, click on the Browse button.

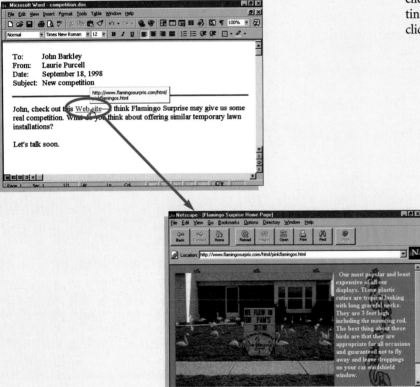

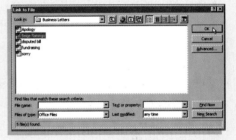

4 In the Link to File dialog box, locate and select the document you want to link to, and click on OK.

5 The path and file name are now displayed in the Link to File or URL text box. Optionally, use the Named Location in File text box to specify what part of the document you want to link to. Examples of named locations include a bookmark in a Word document or a named range in an Excel spreadsheet. (Refer to online help in Word or Excel if you need more help with this.) Then click on OK to return to your document.

A scathing indictment, but not without merit. Overzealous telemarketers, numerous problems with the billing system, personnel turnover, and the infamous "beige flamingo" incident conspired to make last year a service nightmare. (If you like, you can review our response to the beige flamingo complaint.)
Happily, we have turned the corner, and this report will detail the steps we have

D:\Business Letters\Beige flamingo.doc

6 The text you selected in step 1 is now a hyperlink. When you point to it, the mouse pointer becomes a hand, and a ScreenTip lists the name of the destination file or URL. Click on the link to jump to the destination.

How to Convert a Word Document to a Web Page

Underlying every Web page is a plain text file with formatting instructions for the text, graphics, and links. This file is called the *HTML source,* because the instructions are written using the Hypertext Markup Language (HTML). When you convert a Word document to a Web page, Word creates the HTML source for the new page. Word tries to include codes in the source that closely match the formatting of your Word document. Unfortunately, Word's formatting features are far more sophisticated than HTML formatting, so your Web page may not always meet your expectations. If you want more control over the appearance of your Web pages, you might want to create them from scratch (see the next page).

▶ **To change the title of a Web page, make sure the page is on your screen, and choose File, Properties. Edit the title in the Title text box at the top of the Document Properties dialog box, and click on OK.**

▶ **When a Web page is displayed on your screen, the File, Save As HTML command changes to the Save As Word Document command to let you convert the Web page to a Word document.**

▶ **HTML automatically adds blank lines under paragraphs and headings. Consequently, if you press Enter to create blank lines in a Word document, and then convert the document to a Web page, you will end up with too much white space in your Web page. To avoid this problem, create blank lines in your Word document by adding spacing after each paragraph instead of by pressing Enter. (Choose Format, Paragraph, and increase the Spacing After setting.)**

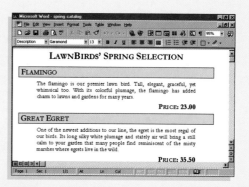

▶ **1** Open the document you want to convert.

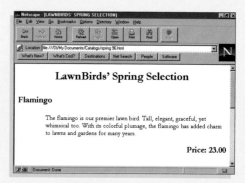

6 Here is the same Web page viewed in the Netscape browser. Depending on how your browser interprets HTML codes, your Web page may look different than it does in Word. (You can quickly display the Web page in your browser by clicking on the Web Page Preview button, which appears in the Standard toolbar—to the right of the Web Toolbar button—when the current document in Word is a Web page.)

2 Choose File, Save As HTML to display the Save As HTML dialog box.

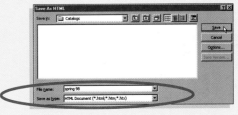

3 Word chooses HTML Document in the Save As Type list. Choose a location for the document in the Save In list, type a name in the File Name text box, and click on the Save button.

A Word document

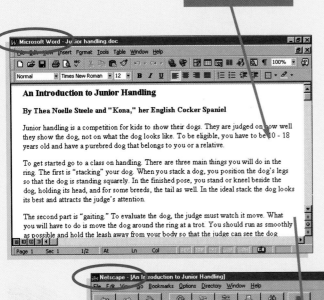

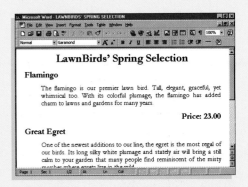

4 Word creates the HTML source behind the scenes, and displays the resulting Web page in the Word window. In this example, Word converted some, but not all of the formatting from the original document.

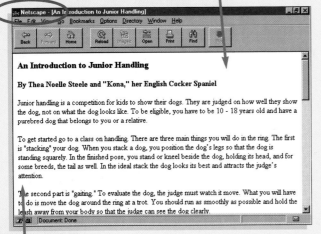

The same document converted to a Web page and viewed in Netscape

5 When Word displays a Web page, it automatically switches to Online Layout view (View, Online Layout) and modifies the menus and toolbars to include commands for working with Web pages. Note that the name displayed in the title bar of a Web page is not the file name, but the title of the document, LAWNBIRDS' SPRING SELECTION in this example. (The Tip Sheet explains how to modify the title.)

How to Create a Web Page

If you want to create an attractive Web page, the best method is to design one from scratch, instead of creating it from a Word document (see the previous page). Word provides two templates for Web pages. The Blank Web Page is a good choice if you already have experience designing Web pages. If, on the other hand, you need a little coaching, the Web Page Wizard is a better option. As with other Wizards, this one asks you some questions, and then handles the formatting and design work for you. All you need to do is fill in the text.

▶ **1** Choose File, New to display the New dialog box.

8 When you have completed the Web page, save it using the File, Save As command. Word automatically chooses HTML Document in the Save As Type list and appends the extension .html to the file name.

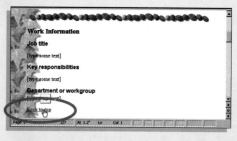

7 After Word jumps to the destination of the link, replace any instructions you find with actual text. (In this example, you'd replace all the [type some text] instructions.) You can also make any changes you'd like to existing text such as the Job title and Key responsibilities headings. To jump quickly back to the top of the Web page, click on the Back to top hyperlink.

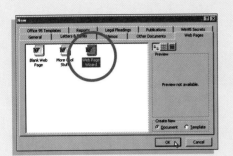

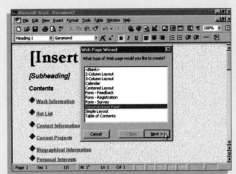

2 Click on the Web Pages tab, click on the Web Page Wizard, and then click on OK.

3 The Web Page Wizard asks what type of Web page you want to create. Try clicking on a few different types. Word shows you a sample of the currently selected type behind the dialog box. In this example, the Wizard will create a personal home page. When you've made your selection, click on the Next button.

> You can use the Web Page Wizard to create Web pages like this one.

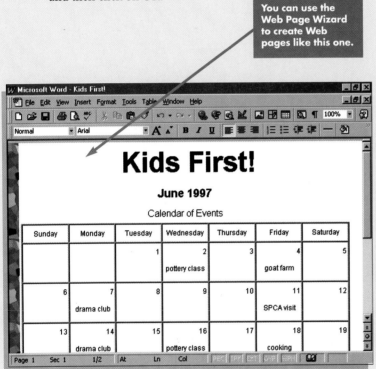

4 Next, the Web Page Wizard asks what style you want. Again, when you click on various options in the list, Word shows you a sample of each style behind the dialog box. Once you've chosen a style (Outdoors in this example), click on the Finish button.

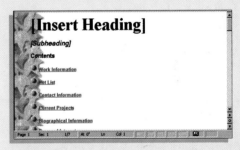

5 Word creates a Web page based on your selections. In this example, the items under—Contents—Work Information, Hot List, Contact Information, and so on—are hyperlinks to other sections of the same Web page. (The status bar indicates that the Web page is 7 pages long.) The placeholder text, [Insert Heading] and [Subheading], shows you where you should type. Select these instructions and type over them with your actual text.

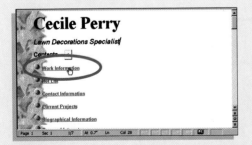

6 To complete the Web page, click on each hyperlink to jump to the various sections, and fill in your text. You can also navigate through the page with the scroll bar or other standard keyboard techniques. Here, clicking on Work Information leads to the Work Information part of the Web page. (The ScreenTip contains the letter A because that's the name Word used in the HTML source to refer to the Work Information section.)

How to Modify a Web Page

Here you learn a few simple ways to spruce up the appearance of a Web page. When you use toolbars, buttons, and menu commands to modify a Web page, Word inserts the appropriate codes in the HTML source. However, each browser recognizes a slightly different set of HTML codes, so there is no guarantee that your page will look the same in a browser as it does in Word. Currently, Netscape and Internet Explorer are the two most popular browsers. If you're going to publish your page on a Web site, open it in both of these browsers to make sure it looks OK before you post it to the site (see the next page).

1 You can easily apply basic character and paragraph formatting to the text in your Web page using buttons in the Formatting toolbar. Begin by selecting the text you want to change.

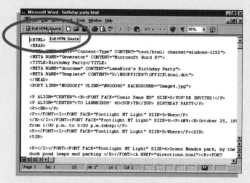

8 Word displays the HTML source code underlying your page. Make the desired changes to the code, save, and then click on the Exit HTML Source button to return to Online Layout view. (If HTML code looks like chicken scratches to you, don't worry. Just use the toolbar buttons and menu commands instead.)

7 If you are familiar with HTML, you might want to edit the HTML source for your page directly so that you can fine-tune the formatting. To do this, choose View, HTML Source. If you have any unsaved changes, Word prompts you to save first before displaying the source.

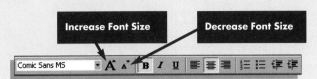

2 Apply changes to the font, font size, font style, alignment, and so on using the Formatting toolbar. When a Web page is displayed in the Word window, Word replaces the Font Size list with the Increase Font Size and Decrease Font Size buttons. Other than that, the buttons for character and paragraph formatting are the same ones that usually appear in the toolbar.

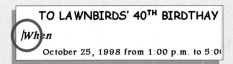

3 To add a horizontal line (also called a horizontal rule) to the page, first place the insertion point where you want to add the line.

4 Then click on the Horizontal Line button in the Formatting toolbar. Word adds a line across the width of the page. To change the line's appearance, right-click on the line and choose Edit AutoShapes from the context menu. Make the desired changes, and click on OK. (If you're editing a Web page you created with the Web Page Wizard, the Horizontal Line button may insert a fancy graphic image instead of a plain line. In this case, you can't edit it as described here.)

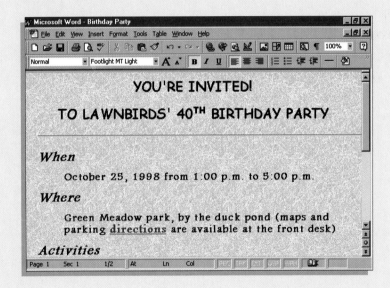

5 To add a background color or texture to the Web page, click on the Fill button in the Formatting toolbar. If you see the color you want in the palette, click on it. Otherwise, choose More Colors to display the Colors dialog box, and choose from a wide range of colors, or choose Fill Effects to display a palette of textures, as shown in the next step.

6 In the Fill Effects dialog box, click on the desired texture, and click on OK.

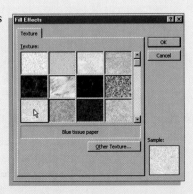

How to Transfer Files via FTP

FTP (File Transfer Protocol) is a protocol you can use to send files between computers on the Internet. Using FTP is a fast and dependable way to download files from other Internet computers. (Computers that offer files for download are called FTP sites.) FTP is also the most convenient way of uploading (or publishing) Web pages you've created to a Web site. To use FTP from Word, you first tell Word about the FTP sites you want to access. Once Word knows about a site, you can use the Open dialog box to download files from the site, and you can use the Save As dialog box to upload files. If you use FTP frequently, you should obtain a more robust and flexible FTP program—a great one to try is CuteFTP (available at http://www.cuteftp.com).

TIP SHEET

▶ As an alternate method of uploading or downloading a file, make sure you've added the site (see steps 1 through 5), and then type the URL for the file in the File Name text box of the Open or Save As dialog box and press Enter. For example, you could display the Open dialog box and type ftp://ftp.albatross.com/update.doc in the File Name text box to download a document called update.doc from the FTP site at albatross.com. (If this is the first time you've connected to this FTP site in this session of Word, you will see the FTP Log On dialog box as described in step 6.)

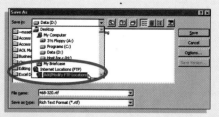

1 To tell Word about an FTP site, first display either the Open or the Save As dialog box. Display the Look In list (in the Open dialog box) or the Save In list (in the Save As dialog box), and click on Add/Modify FTP Locations. This displays the Add/Modify FTP Locations dialog box.

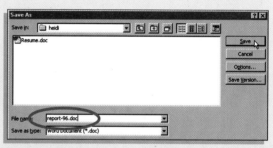

8 If you're downloading a file, click on the file you want to download and click on the Open button. (Word then displays a message box showing you its progress as it downloads the file. After the document appears on your screen, you can use File, Save As to save it onto a local drive.) If you're uploading a file, as shown here, type a name for the file, and click on the Save button.

7 If you aren't already connected to the Internet, you'll see the Connect To dialog box. After you log on, Word connects to the FTP site and displays the folders it contains. Double-click on folders until you display the one you want to upload to or download from is showing in the Look In or Save In list.

3 Many companies let people who don't have personal accounts log in to their FTP site as anonymous users. Anonymous users only have access to certain public areas of a site. Most typically, you connect as an anonymous user if you want to download files—software, graphics, and so on. To add a site you will connect to as an anonymous user (Microsoft's FTP site in this example), enter the name of the site, choose the Anonymous option button, and click on Add.

2 In the Name of FTP Site text box, type the name of the computer at the FTP site, prefaced by ftp. (Just as most Web addresses begin with www, most FTP addresses begin with ftp.) If you aren't sure of the correct name, ask the system administrator at the site. If you don't have a personal account at the FTP site, skip to step 4. If you do, choose the User option button, and enter your user name and password. Then click on the Add button.

4 In this example, two FTP sites have been added to the list of FTP locations at the bottom of the dialog box. When you've finished adding sites, click on OK.

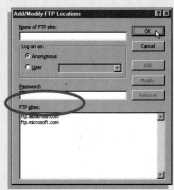

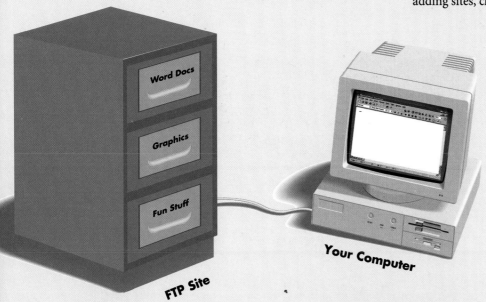

Word Docs

Graphics

Fun Stuff

Your Computer

FTP Site

5 The new FTP locations are now added to the Save In list in the Save As dialog box (and the Look In list in the Open dialog box). Note that Word automatically precedes the addresses with ftp://. To log on to an FTP site, display the Open dialog box to download a file, or the Save As dialog box to upload a file. In the Look In or Save In list, click on the FTP location. In this example, the user will upload (save) a file to the FTP site at albatross.com.

6 Word displays the FTP Log On dialog box and selects the Log on As option based on how you setup the FTP site (see steps 2 and 3). You can change the setting now if you like. If your connecting as an anonymous user, choose Anonymous and click on OK. If you're connecting to a personal account, choose User, type your user name (if necessary) and your password, and click on OK.

INDEX